# Write Web Apps with Dart

**DEVELOP AND DESIGN**

## Jack Murphy

**PEACHPIT PRESS**
WWW.PEACHPIT.COM

**Write Web Apps with Dart: Develop and Design**

Jack Murphy

Peachpit Press
www.peachpit.com

To report errors, please send a note to errata@peachpit.com

Peachpit Press is a division of Pearson Education

Copyright © 2016 by John Murphy

Senior Editor: Karyn Johnson
Development Editor: Robyn G. Thomas
Production Editor: David Van Ness
Copyeditor and Proofreader: Scout Festa
Compositor: Danielle Foster
Indexer: Valerie Haynes Perry
Interior Design: Mimi Heft
Cover Design: Aren Straiger

ISBN-13:  978-0-134-21499-3
ISBN-10:   0-134-21499-4

9 8 7 6 5 4 3 2 1
Printed and bound in the United States of America

*To my charismatic and beautiful wife, Katelyn*

# ACKNOWLEDGMENTS

Behind every author is an amazing team of individuals who provide everything from technical feedback to emotional encouragement.

Writing about a young language and bleeding-edge frameworks definitely didn't make this book easy for anyone. I want to take a moment to thank all the folks from Peachpit Press: Robyn Thomas for providing timely edits and her always kind words, Scout Festa for skillfully editing my text, Cliff Colby for putting this fantastic team together in the first place, and Karyn Johnson for seeing the project over the finish line. And a special thanks goes out to Jonathan Hart for being a consistent questioning voice when providing technical edits and feedback.

On the language side, I want to thank the folks over at Google for developing Dart in the first place. It's such a wonderful language to work with, and the Dart community has been such a welcoming ecosystem to poke around in and learn from. I hope this book helps attract even more Dartisans who can contribute to the vibrant ecosystem.

Finally, I want to thank my new wife for putting up with me writing a book and, at the end, for dealing with me attempting to finish this book the week of our wedding.

# AUTHOR BIO

Jack Murphy is a seasoned start-up technology product- and software-engineering specialist with a full-stack development and UI/UX background. He focuses on front-end client architecture for complex interactive applications. Jack has comprehensive industry experience as a UI-IXD/product designer along with a deep full-stack software engineering expertise.

Jack is currently the vice president of engineering at Augmate, where his team is attempting to facilitate the adoption of wearable technology in enterprise environments. His role allows him to work with numerous types of emerging hardware devices, including smart eyewear, smart watches, and beacon technologies.

Previously, his work focused on browser game development, including *Idle Worship*, *Diner Dash*, and *SmartyCard*. He has passion for design and technology, and he uses both to create rich, engaging, and dynamic user experiences for tech products.

# CONTENTS

## PART I    The Dart Language and Ecosystem

# PART II    Full-Stack App Development with Dart

## ONLINE CHAPTERS

See page xiii in the Introduction for how to access the online chapters.

# INTRODUCTION

Welcome to *Building Web Apps with Dart*. In the following chapters, you will learn all about the Dart language and its extremely powerful ecosystem of community packages.

The goal for this book is to present a series of solutions that a modern full-stack developer will require to become proficient in, and launch a production application with, Dart. Where possible, this book will use code from the Google-backed Dart packages to help ensure the book remains relevant.

For back-end development, I will mirror some of the expected functionality found in many server-side MVC frameworks. For the front end, I will go a step further and not only introduce Dart's built-in front-end tools but also introduce you to Angular 2 Dart for thick-client experiences.

## WHO IS THIS BOOK FOR?

This book assumes you have a novice-level understanding of programming and web application architecture.

You definitely don't need a computer science degree, but I'm assuming that this isn't your first web project. If your experience is strictly from a back-end or non-browser-centric platform, I will introduce many of the primary concepts needed to programmatically interact with the browser.

In addition, this book will introduce you to many of the language features, build tools, and best practices that a developer needs to build a modern web application.

One of the beautiful things about Dart is its similarity to many other C-style languages. If you have spent any time in one of the numerous other C-style languages (Java, JavaScript, Python, and so on), the concepts I discuss should be very familiar. Regardless, I explain the syntax and rules in depth.

This book *is not* a replacement for the low-level Dart API documentation.

## HOW TO USE THIS BOOK

Each section will outline its specific intents and provide step-by-step guides to execute the associated example code. The example code is designed to either illustrate a concept or push forward the example project.

The core of this book is broken into two parts:

- Part I, "The Dart Language and Ecosystem," is a language overview and explains the history of Dart, the core concepts of the Dart language, how to use Dart inside the IntelliJ Community Edition IDE, and the functionality of Dart's task runner, Pub.

  Along the way, you'll learn about the server-side Dart VM, the Dart2JS transpiler, object-oriented programming in Dart, and unique language features to help facilitate asynchronous programming with Dart.

- Part II, "Full-Stack App Development with Dart," takes you through a hands-on approach to building a full-stack application using Dart for both client- and server-side processing. I will cover application planning, the state of database support, Mongo Dart, unit testing, front-end development using only Dart, and finally front-end developing using Angular Dart 2.0.

## FORMATTING

You will see multiple font treatments used to disambiguate different types of content. At a high level, text that is printed in a `monospaced font` refers to code. The following is a high-level breakdown of its uses:

### General code

Blocks of example code appear as follows:

```
function start() {
  print("Hello");
}
```

### Highlighted code

The following style of code is used to draw attention to a concept or to highlight where code has changed:

```
function start() {
  print("Hello World");
}
```

### Code comments

Gray code is used to identify code comments:

```
function start() {
  print("Hello World");  //This is a non-executable comment
}
```

### Code output

If a block of code has output in the Terminal window, it will sometimes be shown as code comments. This will allow you to copy a block of code and ensure that the output matches what's written:

```
function start() {
  print("Output Item A");
  print("Item B");
  print("Item C");
}


//Output Item A
//Item B
//Item C
```

### Command line

Commands that you should run from the Terminal are prefixed with a dollar sign:

```
$ command-to-run
```

### Mongo command line

Commands that you should run from the Mongo client are preceded by an angle bracket:

```
> mongp-command-to-run
```

### Output

Output from any command, either command line or Mongo client, are highlighted as gray, as in the following example:

```
 > mongp-command-to-run
This is output from the mongo database
It is a monospace font and gray


$ terminal-command-to-run
This is output from the terminal
It is a monospace font and gray
```

### Wrapped lines of code

Lines of code that are longer than the printed width of the page allows will wrap to the next line. The wrapped line will be preceded by an arrow to indicate the continued code:

```
main() {
  print( 'Welcome To The City Airport' );
  gotoField(); //Function member of library field –
  ↪ exposed on import field.dart

  //Class Hangar is member of library field
  Hangar aHangar = new Hangar();

  //Class Toolbox is member of library field
  Toolbox portbox = new Toolbox();

}
```

## ONLINE CONTENT

One of the challenges of writing about emerging technology is its propensity to change quickly. In April of 2015, the Dart team announced that the new official front-end framework for Dart is Angular 2.0. Although this is great news for the Dart ecosystem, at the time of this writing the Angular 2 framework is still in its alpha phase of development.

With that news, rather than publishing a book covering stale technology, the decision was made to provide a great opportunity for you to dive head first into the new framework to ensure that you are learning the material that will serve you long term as an active Dartisan.

So the final two chapters will be provided as downloadable PDFs. This means that every reader of this book can log on to peachpit.com and acquire an updated version of the final two chapters, covering Angular 2.0. The updates to the chapters will be available at the following intervals:

- When the book is first published, covering the alpha-level release
- When the beta-level release occurs
- When the final, v2.0.0 release occurs

The rest of the application stack has already been released and is in a mature enough state to put to print. I've used Dart's Pub versioning system to ensure that we have long-term support for the rest of the code in the book.

The following chapters are available from peachpit.com:

- Chapter 16, "Angular Component Implementation and Business Logic"
- Chapter 17, "Deploying to Production Servers"

**To access the *Write Web Apps with Dart* online chapters**, download the files to your computer following these steps:

1. Register your book at www.peachpit.com/register. If you don't already have a Peachpit account, you will be prompted to create one. Once you have an account, you will be prompted to register using the book's ISBN number.
2. Once you are registered at the Peachpit website, click the Account link, select the Registered Products tab, and click the "Access Bonus Content" link.
3. A new page opens with the download files listed. Copy the files to any location you prefer on your system.

## CODE EXAMPLES

As you work through the exercises in this book, you'll encounter all the code that you need to correctly run the examples and compile the projects. However, sometime it's helpful to see the completed output. I've uploaded all the code examples to an active GitHub repository. You can find the code at https://github.com/rightisleft/web_apps_dart.

# WELCOME TO DART

Welcome to Dart! Dart is a powerful, open-source, expressive language for building modern full-stack applications. After reading through this book, you will be able to architect full-stack applications for both front-end and back-end development using Dart. You'll learn how to manage your project using the open-source IntelliJ Community Edition IDE, and you'll manage your application packages and servers using the built-in Pub task runner. Finally, you will spend the last part of the book building a demo Angular 2 Dart application and hosting it in the cloud.

## THE TECHNOLOGIES

The following technologies are all part of your journey into the Dart language.

### DART

Dart is a powerful new language out of Google that enables you to use a single language to target the many facets of a modern web application architecture. Dart ships with a comprehensive SDK that, when paired with the Pub task runner and Pub package manager, will empower you and your team to quickly develop enterprise-level applications for both the web and mobile devices.

### IDEA

JetBrains IDEA Community Edition is an open-source IDE. It has a powerful Dart plugin that provides everything from syntax highlighting and test runners to debuggers and code analysis.

### ANGULAR

Angular is a development framework for building mobile and desktop applications. This book focuses on Angular Dart 2.0. This super-heroic web framework will give you a solid foundation for front-end development using Dart.

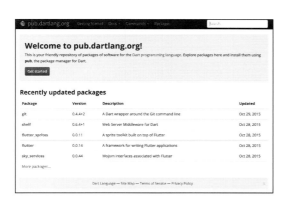

## PUB

Pub is versatile task runner that ships with the Dart SDK. Pub offers developers a standard way to execute a wide range of common tasks, ranging from starting local web servers and acquiring third-party packages to managing version history and running a plethora of custom preprocessors and transformers.

mongoDB

## MONGODB

The Dart community has access to a fantastic project named mongo_dart, which enables the Dart runtime to communicate directly with MongoDB. MongoDB is a document-store style of a NoSQL database that supports a Dart-centric approach to structuring project data.

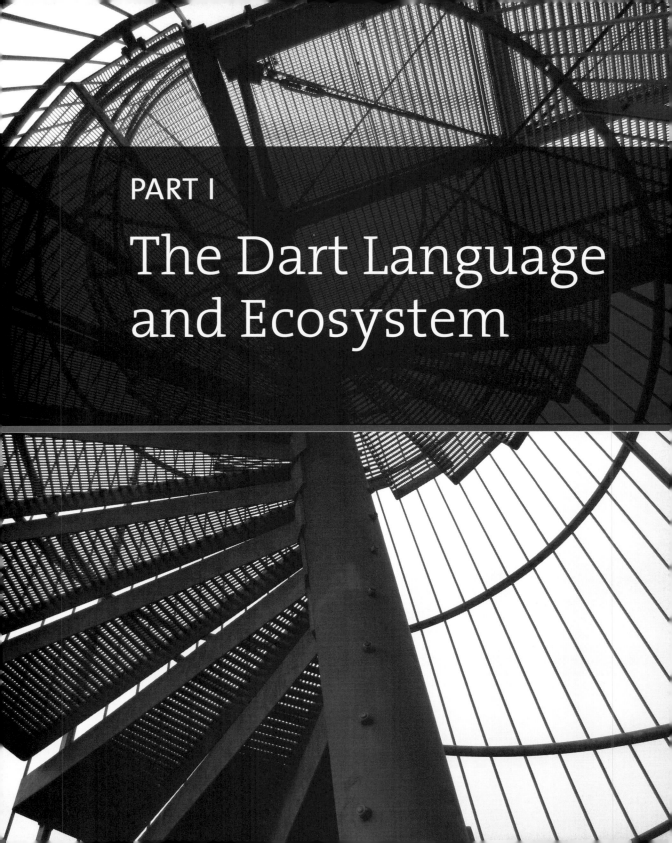

# PART I

# The Dart Language and Ecosystem

# CHAPTER 1

# Dart and the History of Browser Languages

Since the inception of the web browser, browser manufacturers have been struggling to enable all types of authors—from the most brilliant computer science minds in the world to the most timid of technophobes—to publish content on the web. This balancing act resulted in the most diverse, vibrant communication and commerce platform in human history.

In 1995, Netscape Communication Corporation released version 2.0 of its first web browser, known as Netscape Navigator. With this release, it introduced JavaScript to the world.

JavaScript was Netscape's attempt to offer an interpreted programming language with an extremely low barrier to entry. In parallel, Netscape Navigator also shipped with the capability to execute Java applets, enabling authors with a stronger technical background to deploy more sophisticated applications directly in the browser.

This balancing act between power and accessibility continued as the Internet matured into the global marketplace that we know today. These early choices would have long-lasting effects on how software was developed for the web.

# THE WEB AND OPEN STANDARDS

Over the two decades after the release of Netscape, one of the most powerful drivers of technological change to the web was the relentless commitment to open standards. In 1997, Netscape submitted to ECMA International a version of JavaScript that became ECMA-262 specification v1. The political ramifications of adhering to open standards enabled competing browser vendors to develop their own compatible virtual machines (VMs).

The ECMA-262 standard became the language of choice for the web. The upside to having a single language was that web authors had a consistent platform on which to develop their applications, and browser vendors had a single standard on which to optimize their efforts from both software engineering and business strategy perspectives.

The downside to this unified approach has been one-dimensional political behavior among major browser vendors, and it has resulted in an ever-shrinking number of language choices in browsers. At the same time, the number of virtual machines that adhered to the ECMA-262 standard skyrocketed, and competing technologies, such as Java, Flash, and ActiveX, despite sometimes having significant performance upsides, were deemed incompatible or insecure or branded as obsolete. The deprecation of these alternatives was often based not solely on technical merit but on battles over market position.

# JAVASCRIPT DEFICITS

The dichotomy between the need for power and the need for accessibility in a web programming language is nuanced, and the importance of either is often calculated based on the needs and experience of the author. With the increased demands placed on modern web applications and the removal of competing language options, many are taking a critical eye to the inherent flaws in JavaScript.

Even the most ardent JavaScript enthusiast advocates understanding its most common pitfalls. At a high level, some of these critiques include weak typing, no true hash map, limited numerical types, prototypical inheritance, falsy values, unexpected this behavior, odd equality operators, and misleading applications of new factory methods.

Problems that are often manageable in small amounts have a compounding effect at scale; JavaScript is not immune to this. Things that might be trivial to solve on a small web project can grind an enterprise development process to a crawl.

# MODERN ALTERNATIVES

With only one language to use on the web platform, the development community has created a plethora of JavaScript transpilers that aim to address many of the shortcomings of JavaScript. Each of these projects often starts with the goal of addressing what the author sees as the most egregious offenses in the JavaScript language:

- **CoffeeScript** takes aim at JavaScript's C-style syntax.
- **TypeScript** is Microsoft's attempt to add optional static typing.
- **Emscripten** allows developers to port code from C, C++, or any project with LLVM byte code onto the web.
- **asm.js** is a subset of the JavaScript language that is highly optimizable and geared for performance.

The most notable transpiler at the time of this writing is Microsoft's TypeScript. TypeScript is a strict superset of JavaScript, with its biggest emphasis being optional static typing. All these libraries have achieved moderate success because, while offering very different high-level language options, the final output is capable of running across all major browsers when transpiled to JavaScript.

# ECMASCRIPT 4

One of the more successful competitors to JavaScript has always been the Flash VM and its ActionScript language. The platform was a popular target for rich Internet application developers because of the feature-rich language, excellent asset pipeline tooling, and consistent interface to underlying video and audio hardware layers.

ActionScript 3 was Adobe's attempt to tool its family of web products with a next-generation language that addressed many of the issues of the ECMA-262 standard. Adobe used ActionScript 3 as the foundation for its draft proposal of the ECMA-262 v4 standard, along with its open source Tamarin virtual machine. In effect, the ECMA-262 v4 draft was an effort to correct the many deficiencies JavaScript had suffered from and an opportunity for the entire industry to put an improved technology into the hands of the public.

At the time of the ECMA TC39 committee meeting in Oslo in 2008, Microsoft's Internet Explorer still maintained roughly 80 percent market share among web browsers. The ECMA TC39 group was composed of members representing Google, Mozilla, Microsoft, Adobe, and other vendors. Microsoft aggressively argued against v4 of the standard, and instead advocated for the ECMA-262 v3.1 standard, which was an incremental enhancement and more in line with their current product offerings. After years of the group being split, and a process "mired in a morass of bickering, infighting, and sometimes, out and out name calling" (https://blogs.adobe.com/open/2008/08), the group agreed to move forward with the more conservative v3.1.

This essentially left Adobe, and the software industry at large, holding a technology that was politically dead in the water despite having sound technological upsides. ECMAScript v4 advocates had no way to target browsers that they did not have direct control over, and were faced with a political and market environment that was not going to back their efforts. This was an important lesson for browser vendors looking to introduce meaningful change into the browser landscape in the future.

## DASH MEMO

In 2010, roughly two years after the defeat of ECMAScript 4, an internal Google memo, commonly referred to as the "Dash memo," was leaked to the web. In this memo, Google outlined a "2 pronged" (http://pastebin.com/NUMTTrKj) approach to language tooling in the browser.

The first approach Google outlined was considered a "low risk/low reward" (http://pastebin.com/NUMTTrKj) approach that involved continued support for the evolving ECMAScript v6 standard. The downside of this approach was the continued sluggish pace of uptake by the remainder of the industry. In addition, even with the eventual adoption of newer language features, this approach would continue to inherit the core language issues that are at the heart of ECMAScript.

The second approach Google outlined was referred to as a "high risk/high reward" (http://pastebin.com/NUMTTrKj) strategy. This was a radical departure from the ECMAScript standard and a rethinking of how a web language should be designed. It was to be a new a language that maintained the low barrier to entry that JavaScript enjoyed, with the power, maintainability, and tooling of a modern high-level programming language. This language would go on to become Dart.

# GOOGLE'S MARKET STRATEGY

Google learned a lot from watching the defeat of ECMAScript v4. Google executed a technology strategy that ensured it didn't need consensus from the browser vendors prior to getting its language to market. To do this, Google's new Dart language runs on all major browsers right out of the gate. It accomplishes this by introducing three new pieces of technology alongside the Dart language: the Dart2JS transpiler, the Dart Dev Compiler, and the open source Dart virtual machine (VM).

## DART2JS

Dart2JS is a transpiler that takes Dart code and outputs backward-compatible optimized JavaScript. This works on most modern browsers, including Chrome, Firefox, Safari, and Internet Explorer 9+.

The transpiler runs as a pre-processor that outputs minified JavaScript that can be executed inside most JavaScript virtual machines. The compilation step not only translates Dart code into compact, highly performant JavaScript, but also takes it through a process called *tree shaking*. Tree shaking analyzes your source code and removes any unused portions. This attempts to ensure that all the shipped code is actually being used. Dart2JS has been developed alongside the Dart VM and has been considered production ready since version 1.

## DART DEV COMPILER

In addition to Dart2JS, the Dart team is working on a new piece of technology named the Dart Dev Compiler (DDC). The DDC aims to address some of the complexity that has resulted from having highly optimized JavaScript code as the output from Dart2JS; namely, readability of the code.

The DDC aims to output human-readable JavaScript. This will enable developers to use Dart and its powerful ecosystem of development tools to write, test, and maintain public native JavaScript libraries. The DDC is also an intermediary debugging tool that will allow developers to run Dart code as readable native JavaScript in all major browsers. This will emulate the experience of how the app will function after Dart2JS transpiles the language while maintaining readability for debugging. The DDC is slated to be released alongside Dart SDK 2.0 in early 2016; however, the project is currently hosted publicly and available for preview at https://pub.dartlang.org/packages/dev_compiler.

## DART VIRTUAL MACHINE

The Dart VM is core to Google's Dart initiative and exists to power server-side development needs. It incorporates many language features found in other server-side languages and pairs them with the ability to share libraries between your back-end and front-end applications.

Google assigned the development of this VM to an engineer with a long history of building highly performant VMs: Lars Bak. Bak was the core architectural contributor to many notable high performance VMs, including the Java VM and Google's own V8 JavaScript VM.

The Dart VM is specifically optimized for the Dart language. Google optimized performance for a single language instead of making a more generic bytecode compilation target. Having a language VM allows for direct interpretation and execution of Dart source code by the VM without the need for a compilation step. Compilation into machine code is achieved using a JIT compiler that interprets the code at run time.

The Dart VM runs on an event loop with two queues: an event queue and a microtask queue. This enables the Dart VM to implement non-blocking asynchronous operations. The Dart VM is single threaded, which offers a straightforward developer debugging environment. However, to take advantage of multi-core architectures, Dart also supports isolates, or "isolated memory heaps." Each isolate has its own event loop. The Dart VM and its corresponding isolate terminate when both queues are empty.

The Dart VM supports two different run-time modes. The first run-time mode is referred to as *checked mode*. Checked mode relies on the language's support for optional typing. This allows developers to test their code and to have the language fail fast and loud when the wrong object type is encountered.

The second of Dart's run-time modes is called *production mode*. This mode is optimized for performance and not for developer feedback. Surprisingly, while in production mode, the Dart VM initially ignores all the author-assigned object types. Instead, the Dart VM heavily uses polymorphic inline caching to improve VM performance. Dart sees much of its performance gains over ECMAScript VMs by adding support for additional primitives, which yields more accurate heuristics when executing its inline cache functionality. The VM also leverages rigid object structures that are exposed by having native class support in the language. Google's documentation shows significant speed gains by the Dart VM when compared to Google's own V8 JavaScript VM.

## DART VIRTUAL MACHINE STRATEGY

For many years, Google advocated for Dart VM to sit alongside JavaScript inside Chrome and other browsers. Google tried to work with other manufacturers to solicit interest in the technology. The team even had long-running experimental support for the VM in Dartium, a branch of its Chromium browser.

However, after years of active development, Google decided not to pursue an alternative VM in the browser. Instead, Google decided to follow the increasing trend of using JavaScript as a compilation target while in the browser.

As the ECMAScript standard has improved, the capacity to use JavaScript as an assembly-like language for the web has become more and more viable. This means developers can get all the great language tooling from Dart and maintain the cross-browser compatibility that ECMAScript enjoys today.

The Dart VM, while not being deployed in the browser, is still under heavy development by Google for mobile and server-side applications. Developers can write and deploy highly performant production applications by using the Dart VM and its associated server-side libraries.

**NOTE:** If you're interested in seeing Dart benchmarks when compared to platforms like Nodejs or Rails, take a look at the EC2 hardware tests at www.techempower.com/benchmarks/#section=data-r10&hw=ec2&test=json.

## HOW IS THE DART LANGUAGE DIFFERENT?

The Dart language is Google's attempt to deliver a better experience than ECMAScript. So what does it look like? The next few chapters will dive deep into Dart's many language features, but here are a few of the high-level features:

- **Syntax:** Dart supports a familiar syntax that's similar to Java, C, C#, or JavaScript, with additional semantics inspired by Smalltalk to enable terse, concise code.

- **Sane scope and contexts:** Dart follows traditional lexical scoping rules with hierarchical scope. Children inherit their parent's scope, but parents cannot access their child's scope. Class methods have a consistent reference to the instance using the this keyword.

- **Single consistent entry point:** All Dart applications start with a named function, main(), that establishes the run-time context from the rest of the application.

- **Access modifiers:** Dart supports public and private members, allowing authors to properly encapsulate object access as they see fit.

- **Optional static types:** At its core, Dart is a dynamic language. However, the Dart VM and the IDE provide optional static typing. Typed objects produce more readable code and provide type checking during execution.

- **Classical inheritance and more:** Dart supports classical single inheritance. In Dart, a class can be used as a class, an interface, or a mixin.

  Dart also supports abstract methods, abstract classes, and interfaces. You can use these structural elements to define shared interfaces in which individual classes can then implement their own solutions. These are language features that are often used when creating contemporary object-oriented (OO) relationships.

- **Mixins:** Mixins allow you to append previously implemented methods to classes without using inheritance.
- **Multiple numeric types:** Dart has built-in support for two types of numerical objects with a more generic parent class.
  - `int`: A signed integer with a max range of 53 bits.
  - `double`: A data type representing an IEEE-754 double-precision floating-point number.
  - `num`: A generic superclass for class `double` and class `int`. A `num` can be either.
- **Built-in library support:** Importing a library is a way to bring a cohesive collection of classes and methods into the current scope. By default, the `dart:core` library is automatically imported into every Dart program. `dart:core` provides many of the building blocks needed to implement the most common programming tasks. You can also define your own libraries and share them with your team or publicly.
- **Built-in package support:** A *package* is a collection of libraries, classes, and methods that work in unison. Your main application is a package, but it can consist of many other packages. Packages can be easily acquired or shared using the Pub repository.
- **Pub:** While not part of the language specification, Pub is a tool that is central to the propagation of Dart code. Pub is part task runner, part package manager. Pub can download packages, manage server state, execute compilation tasks, and much more.

## A NEW ECMA STANDARD

From the outset, Google has positioned Dart to be open. The Dart VM is open source. The core packages are open source. And while the engineering team over at Google was busy working on the Dart VM, the ECMA TC52 committee, with representatives from Google, was busy defining a new standard. In July of 2014, ECMA International announced that ECMA-408 had officially been approved for the Dart Programming Language Specification. The specification was based on the Dart VM 1.3 instruction set. The standard is now open to anyone who wants to target it.

## SUMMARY

With Dart, you now have a language that works on both client and server. It is backward compatible with most major browsers. It doesn't break any existing standards. It adheres to a new open standard. It has an open-sourced VM.

I firmly believe that Dart has huge potential to change how the software industry handles large-scale applications development for the web, and I think you're going to really enjoy working with it.

### YOU SHOULD KNOW:

- Where JavaScript came from
- Why Dart was invented
- Why designing a one-size-fits-all web language is challenging
- What a transpiler is
- What a virtual machine is
- Where and how Dart can be run
- What Dart's language feature set includes

# CHAPTER 2

# Up and Running with Dart

Before you dive into the Dart language, you need to get the Dart run-time environments set up on your computer. This chapter covers how to execute Dart code both on the command line and in-browser.

You'll be working with the Dart SDK and JetBrains' IntelliJ IDEA Community Edition. As with most languages, there are multiple ways to get Dart up and running on your workstation. These approaches vary based on whether you are running Windows, Linux, or Mac OS X. The good news is that the tooling support for each operating system is excellent.

IntelliJ IDEA Community Edition is the open-source variant of JetBrains' powerful collection of full-featured IDEs. The Dart team has selected the software company JetBrains to provide the editor of choice for the Dart community. Previously, the folks over at Google provided their own editor, named Dart Editor. Dart Editor was deprecated in the summer of 2015.

Dart Editor was built using the Eclipse software development kit (SDK), which provided many of the workspace, plugin, and debugging capabilities found in other enterprise-level software development tools. In order to ensure the widest range of choice for developers, Google decided to focus its energy on making available all the plugins that were used in Dart Editor as standalone plugins that could be leveraged by any IDE. This approach now enables Dart support on a wide range of IDEs, such as Sublime, Eclipse, eMac, vim, IntelliJ, and many more.

The remainder of this book uses the open-source IntelliJ IDEA Community Edition editor.

## INSTALLING THE DART SDK

Let's walk through how to acquire the Dart SDK for your specific operating system. Here's how to grab the files for your machine.

**NOTE:** The steps in this section include a USER_HOME placeholder in italic. You should replace USER_HOME with the proper path of your operating system's designated user folder. For example, my system username is jmurphy. On OS X, the steps show /Users/*USER_HOME*/projects, but I'll enter the path as /Users/jackmurphy/projects/.

1. Go to www.dartlang.org/downloads/archive.
2. Under the Stable Channel heading, ensure that the latest version is selected in the drop-down menu. You will need to use version 1.12 or greater.
3. Select your operating system from the drop-down menu.
4. Click Dart SDK for the appropriate 32-bit or 64-bit architecture of your workstation. This will download the compressed Dart SDK.
5. Click Dartium for the appropriate 32-bit or 64-bit architecture of your workstation. This will download the compressed Dartium Browser.

**NOTE:** At the time of this writing, Windows and OS X have only a 32-bit version of Dartium available. Please use the 32-bit version.

6. Uncompress the downloaded SDK file to expose a folder named dart-sdk.

7. Place `dart-sdk` in one of the following folders, based on your operating system. When working on your own projects, you can place the `dart-sdk` folder in the location of your choice.
   - Windows: `C:\Users\`*USER_HOME*`\dart-sdk`
   - OS X and Linux: `/Users/`*USER_HOME*`/dart-sdk`

8. Uncompress the downloaded Dartium file to expose a folder named something like `dartium-os-full-stable`.

9. Place `dartium-os-full-stable` in one of the following folders, based on your operating system. When working on your own projects, you can place the `dartium-os-full-stable` folder in the location of your choice.
   - Windows: `C:\Users\`*USER_HOME*`\dartium-os-full-stable`
   - OS X and Linux: `/Users/`*USER_HOME*`/dartium-os-full-stable`

## WHAT'S IN THE DART-SDK

The `dart-sdk` contains several folders, files, applications, and more:

- `bin` contains executable files for developing with Dart.
    - `dart` is the Google Dart VM.
    - `dart2js` is the Dart JavaScript transpiler.
    - `dartanalyzer` is a Dart static analysis tool.
    - `dartdocgen` is a generator to turn comments into documentation.
    - `dartfmt` is a Dart code formatter.
    - `docgen` is a legacy document generator.
    - `pub` is a Dart task runner and package manager.
    - `snapshots` are stored memory snapshots of byte data to help Dart start up faster.
- `lib` is a folder that contains the primary libraries that make up the Dart run time.
- `revision` is a file that contains the SDK version number.
- `version` is a file that contains source control information.

# DART ENVIRONMENTAL VARIABLES

The Dart SDK binaries should be part of your system's default environment path. If you are not using a package manager, you will need to add the file system location of the `dart-sdk` folder to your existing environmental variables. Each operating system variant has a different way to persist environment variables; the following sections contain a few recommendations.

## WINDOWS 8

If you're setting up your development environment on a Windows 8 operating system, use the following instructions:

1. In the search bar, search for Advanced System Settings, and click the corresponding icon to open the System Properties dialog.
2. While under the Advanced tab, click the Environment Variables button.
3. Under the System Variables section, double-click the Path system variable.
4. Append the following new semicolon-delimited value to the end of the existing string:

   ```
   ;C:\Users\USER_HOME\dart-sdk\bin\
   ```
5. Save, and restart Windows to make the changes take effect.
6. Open a new command-line session, and execute the following code in the terminal:

   ```
   $ dart --version
   ```

   The following will display:

   ```
   Dart VM version: 1.12.xxx
   ```

## MAC OS X 10.10

If you are running OS X 10.10, you will need to append the path of your Dart binaries to the /etc/paths file.

1. Open your terminal, and execute the following command:

   ```
   $ printf "\n/Users/USER_HOME/dart-sdk/bin" | sudo tee -a /etc/paths
   ```
2. Open a new command-line session, and execute the following code in the terminal:

   ```
   $ dart --version
   ```

   The following will display:

   ```
   Dart VM version: 1.12.xxx
   ```

## UBUNTU 14.10

If you're setting up your development environment on an Ubuntu 14.10 operating system, use the following instructions:

1. Open Terminal.
2. Run the following command:

   ```
   $ sudo nano /etc/environment
   ```

**NOTE:** You need the root password to launch the nano editor for this file.

3. In the nano editor, append the following new colon-delimited value to the end of the existing path string:

   ```
   :/Users/USER_HOME/dart-sdk/bin
   ```

4. Run the following command:

   ```
   $ source /etc/environment
   ```

5. Open a new command-line session, and execute the following code in the terminal:

   ```
   $ dart --version
   ```

   The following will display:

   ```
   Dart VM version: 1.12.xxx
   ```

# INTELLIJ IDEA EDITOR

IntelliJ IDEA is an extremely feature-rich IDE, including syntax highlighting, interactive debugging, pub integration, source control, built-in file management, and more. The rest of this book explores much of its functionality. Rather than diving right into language specifics, let's take Dart out for a test drive. The goal over the next few sections is to introduce you to the Dart command line, Dart code interpretation in Dartium, and Dart2JS compiled code.

> **NOTE:** The convention this book uses is to store packages in a folder named projects in your user home folder. The book conventions use POSIX file system semantics, so if you are on Windows, please adjust accordingly.

## INSTALLING IDEA FOR DART

At the time of this writing, IntelliJ Community Edition does not include Dart by default. If you're OK with proprietary software, JetBrains' WebStorm IDE ships with Dart support built in. WebStorm also ships with excellent support for many other web languages, such as JavaScript, CSS, SASS, YAML, and more.

That being said, it is very simple to add support for the Dart language to the Community Edition. Let's walk through acquiring the open-source version of JetBrains' IntelliJ IDEA editor:

1. In your browser, go to www.jetbrains.com/idea/download.
2. Click Download Community to download the installer.
3. Run the downloaded installer, named ideaIC-##.#.# (where ##.#.# is the version number).
4. Launch the IntelliJ IDEA CE application.

**FIGURE 2.1**
Configuration
options on the IntelliJ
Welcome screen

**FIGURE 2.2**
Dart plugin panel

5. Select any options that you find to your liking.

   Each operating system has its own unique set of customization options. For this project, you do not need to select any additional options that are not already selected by default.

   Upon finishing customization, you'll see the IntelliJ Welcome screen (**Figure 2.1**).

6. In the lower-right corner, click the Configure menu and select Plugins from the drop-down menu.

7. Enter **Dart** in the search field in the upper-left corner, then click the Browse Repositories button (**Figure 2.2**).

   A new window will pop up with a Dart plugin panel exposed.

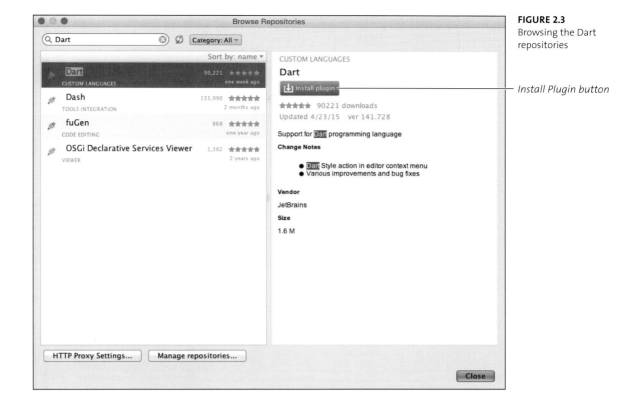

**FIGURE 2.3**
Browsing the Dart
repositories

*Install Plugin button*

8. Click the green Install Plugin button (**Figure 2.3**).

   When the install is complete, a dialog window will open and ask you to restart IDEA.

9. Click the Restart button, and wait for IDEA to reboot. Dart language support and tooling is now enabled via a plugin for the IDEA IDE on your machine.

## RUNNING DART

One of the compelling aspects of Dart is its ability to execute code on multiple platforms. You can run your libraries as server code, as client code, or on mobile. Let's take a look at a few different ways to get your code up and running.

### COMMAND-LINE APPLICATIONS

Command-line applications run the Dart VM as a headless process on a server. In this case, the server is your local development workstation. Let's take a look at how to launch your application through the IDEA.

1. Open IntelliJ IDEA.

2. Select File > New Project, or click Create New Project on the Welcome splash screen.

3. On the left panel, select Dart.

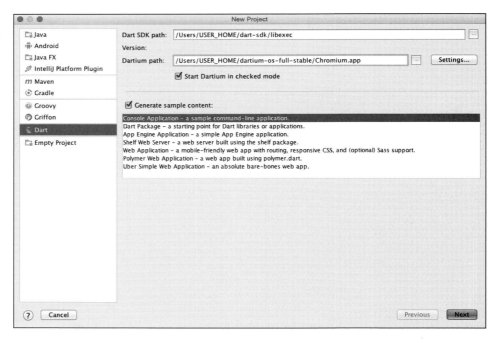

4. Enter the following values in the New Project dialog (**Figure 2.4**):
   - Dart SDK Path: **/Users/*USER_HOME*/dart-sdk/libexec**
   - Dartium Path: **/Users/*USER_HOME*/dartium-os-full-stable/Chromium.app**
5. Select the Generate Sample Content checkbox.
6. Select the Console Application entry in the list of sample content.
7. Click Next, and enter the following values:
   - Project Name: **dart_console_temp**
   - Project Location: **/Users/*USER_HOME*/projects/dart_console_temp**

   IntelliJ will generate a project scaffold that will be visible in the Projects panel in a folder named dart_console_temp. This scaffold will contain all the files needed to run a command-line Dart application. Let's go ahead and run it.
8. In the window bar, select Run > Edit Configurations.

   In the new dialog (**Figure 2.5**), you'll see a panel on the left side with a plus icon above it.
9. Click the plus icon, and select Dart Command Line App.
10. Name the new configuration **DartConsole**.
11. Click the ellipses button to the right of the Dart File field, and find bin/main.dart in the active project.
12. Click the ellipses button to the right of the Working Directory field, and select the folder dart_console_temp.

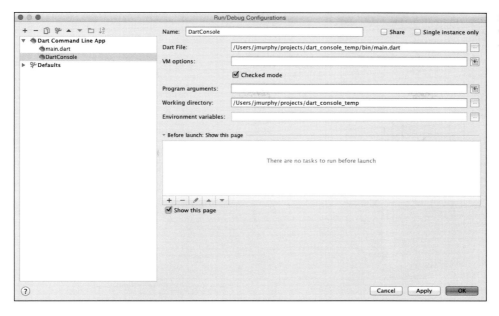

FIGURE 2.5
Configuring the run
and debug options

13. Click OK to save, and close your configuration.

14. In the top menu bar, choose Run > Run 'DartConsole'.

In the console, you should see the following output:

```
Hello World: 42!
```

Let's review what you just did:

First, any file can be an application entry point file for a package. You can name it whatever you prefer. Dart does require an initial function named `main()` to be implemented in the chosen file. In the sample package, the scaffolded template has the application entry point file named `main.dart` that contains a function named `main()`.

Secondly, IntelliJ created a run configuration for your command-line app. By defining `main.dart` as the Dart file value, you're telling the IntelliJ to have the Dart VM interpret and execute `main.dart`. IntelliJ can have multiple launchers for a single package.

You can get the same results executing code on the command line using the Dart VM.

15. Open your terminal, and type the following:

```
$ cd /Users/USER_HOME/projects/dart_console_temp
$ dart bin/main.dart
```

You'll see the following output in the terminal:

```
Hello world: 42!
```

You are temporarily finished with the `dart_console_temp` application.

16. Close the project by choosing File > Close Project.

**FIGURE 2.6**
The New Project
dialog for a Dart web
application

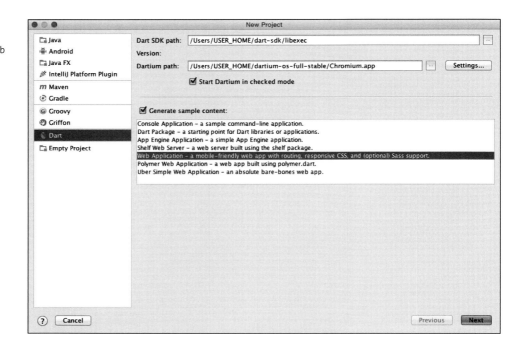

### WEB APPLICATIONS IN DARTIUM

Let's head back to the IntelliJ IDEA and create a client web application with a pre-built interface.

1. If needed, open IntelliJ IDEA.
2. Select File > New Project, or click the Create New Project button on the splash screen.
3. In the new window, in the left panel, select Dart.
4. Enter the following values in the New Project dialog (**Figure 2.6**):
   - Dart SDK Path: **/Users/***USER_HOME***/dart-sdk/libexec**
   - Dartium Path: **/Users/***USER_HOME***/dartium-os-full-stable/Chromium.app**
5. Select the Generate Sample Content checkbox.
6. Select Web Application from the list of sample content projects.
7. Click Next, and enter the following values:
   - Project Name: `dart_web_temp`
   - Project Location: **/Users/***USER_HOME***/projects/dart_web_temp**
8. Click Finish.

   IntelliJ will generate another project scaffold that will be visible in the Project panel in a folder titled dart_web_temp. This scaffold will contain all the files needed to run a sample web application powered by Dart.

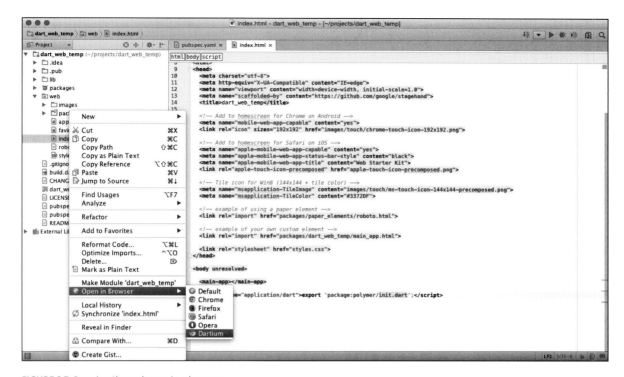

**FIGURE 2.7** Running the webpage in a browser

9. In the Project panel (**Figure 2.7**), select the web folder. Right-click index.html, and choose Open in Browser > Dartium.

   You should see an instance of Chromium launch and a simple webpage render. You now have front-end and back-end code powered by Dart.

10. Type **Dartisan** into the input field on the launched webpage. Ensure that you see the input string rendered in reverse below the input field: nasitraD.

    Let's take a look at what happened.

    You may have noticed that the index.html file you specified is being hosted on a web server at the address http://localhost:63342/. This is IntelliJ's built-in web server.

    Dart has a companion task runner named Pub. Pub is shipped with an HTTP server to allow you to run a Dart server instance. When you start the IntelliJ web server, it also spawns an instance of the Pub HTTP server on a port within the range of 40000–59999.

    By default, the raw Pub server will expose the optional child folders of /web, /test, and /lib. This example uses only:

    ~/projects/dart_web_temp/web/

    ~/projects/dart_web_temp/lib/

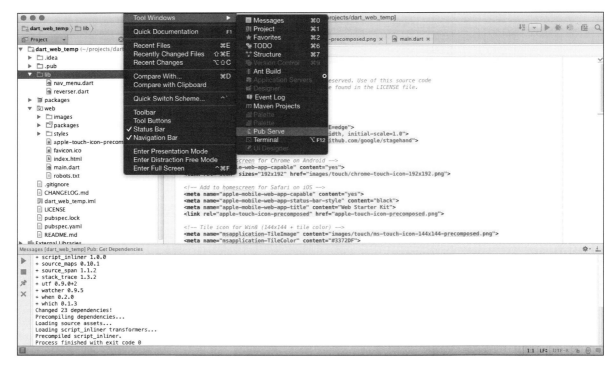

**FIGURE 2.8** Accessing Pub Serve

Because Dartium is running with the included Dart VM, `main.dart` is interpreted directly in the browser by the Dart VM. The browser uses an HTML5-compliant script tag to pass `main.dart` to the Dart VM. This works in exactly the same way as passing a JavaScript file to the V8 VM. Let's take a look at the source code in the browser.

11. In the Dartium top menu, select View > Developer > Developer Tools.

12. In the new panel, click Sources.

You should see the code from `main.dart` with content from your `lib` folder. You can add breakpoints and step through your Dart code the same way you would a JavaScript file in the developer tools.

Next, we'll kill the running instance of the Pub HTTP server.

13. Return to IntelliJ.

14. In the top menu bar, choose View > Tool Windows > Pub Serve (**Figure 2.8**).

15. Click the red icon labeled Stop Pub Serve.

Although it's convenient to launch the server from IntelliJ, you can also launch the HTTP server from the command line.

16. Open your terminal and type the following:

```
$ cd /Users/USER_HOME/projects/dart_web_temp/
$ pub serve
```

17. Go to http://localhost:8080 in Chromium to load a new instance of our web application.

    While the page is loading, you'll see log statements from the Pub HTTP server in your console. This will bypass the built-in IntelliJ proxy server and use the HTTP server from Pub directly.

18. With the console selected, press Control-C to kill the server instance.

## WEB APPLICATIONS IN CONTEMPORARY BROWSERS

Being able to execute Dart code through the Dart VM directly in a Chrome variant is powerful. It's a great tool for writing and debugging your code, but you probably want to ship your product on popular browsers. Let's take a look at running your Dart code in a browser that has mass adoption. Let's test in Chrome, but this will also work in Safari, Firefox, or Internet Explorer.

You can use the same dart_web_temp package that you made in the last section. But let's launch it in Chrome.

1. In IDEA, in the Project panel, select the web folder. Right click index.html, and choose Open in Browser > Chrome.

    The application will launch an instance of your system's Chrome browser. The browser URL will be something like http://localhost:63342/dart_web_temp/web/index.html. Again, this is the IntelliJ server proxying the Pub HTTP server.

    If you type **Dartisan** in the input box, it will be reversed just as in the previous section. How does this work if your Chrome browser doesn't have a Dart VM?

2. Open Firefox, and go to the generated address from the Chrome URL bar in step 1.

3. In the Text Input field, type **Dartisan**.

4. Verify that the reversed word functionality works as it did in Chrome.

5. Close Firefox.

    When you make a request to launch your application in Chrome, IntelliJ starts a new instance of the HTTP server via Pub. The Pub HTTP server has the capacity to execute a conditional series of transformers to prepare your assets.

    The web project scaffold ships with a small JavaScript library, named dart.js, that is loaded into index.html. If the caller is not a Dart-compatible browser, the library makes a request to the HTTP server, which will transpile the Dart code on demand and respond with a JavaScript file that gets loaded into the page.

Transformers are libraries that can preprocess assets prior to serving the HTTP response. One of those transformers is the Dart2JS transpiler. Dart2JS is bundled as a transformer that is executed by the web server when the client requests a JavaScript file that also maps to an application entry point of a Dart library.

On request, the Dart2JS transformer serves up a concatenated, transpiled JavaScript file with the name of the original entry point. In this case it's named `main.dart.js`. This JavaScript file can be executed in most modern browsers.

## LINE NUMBERS

Showing or hiding line numbers is a matter of personal preference. I prefer to have them on and will be making reference to them throughout the book. Showing them is a simple process.

1. In the top menu of the IntelliJ editor, click IntelliJ IDEA.
2. Click Preferences.
3. Choose Editor > General > Appearance.
4. Under the Appearance section, click Show Line Numbers.
5. Click OK to save.

   You should now see line numbers on all open documents.

## DART COMMAND LINE DEBUGGER

One of the more useful features of a full-featured IDE is the debugger. IntelliJ has an extremely powerful debugger built in. Let's take it for a test drive.

1. If your web project is open, choose File > Close Project.
2. At the Welcome screen, select `dart_console_temp` to open the previous project.
3. In the Project panel, toggle open the folder `dart_console_temp`, and toggle open the folder `lib`.
4. Double-click the `dart_console_temp.dart` file to open it in the editor.
5. Change the function `calculate()` to the following:

   ```
   int calculate() {
     var firstResult = 6 * 7;
     var secondResult = firstResult * 2;
     return firstResult;
   }
   ```
6. Open the ~/dart_console_temp/bin/main.dart file.
7. Place your cursor on the line beginning with `Hello World` (line 7).

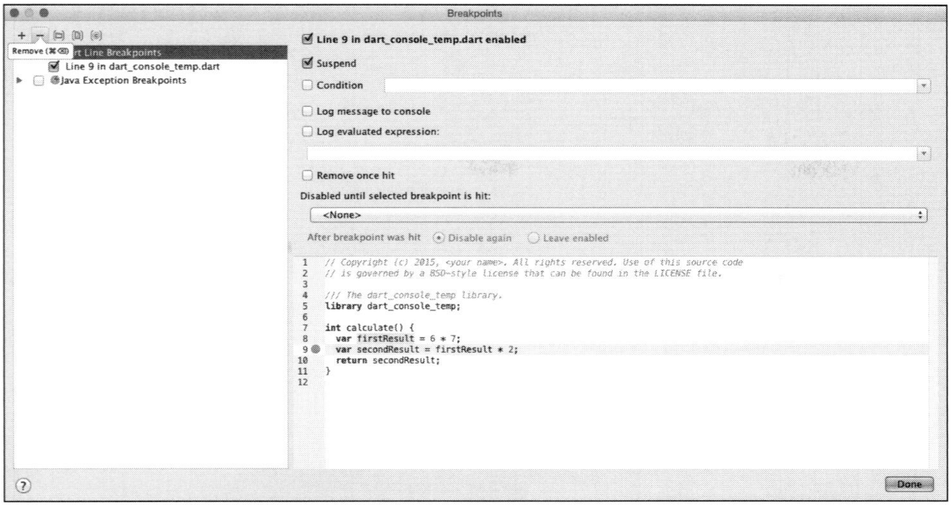

**FIGURE 2.9**
Removing breakpoints

8. Press Command-F8 to place a breakpoint. This is indicated by a red dot to the left of the line.

9. In the menu bar, choose Run > Debug. In the dialog window, choose main.dart.

   IntelliJ will stop execution with the breakpoint line highlighted. Dart VM has paused execution on the selected line. In the various IntelliJ panels, you can explore the current run-time state of the objects in your application.

10. Press F7 to step into the function.

    This will move the execution context into the `calculate()` function from the highlighted line and pause the VM for further inspection.

11. Press F8 to step over a function.

    This will execute the highlighted line and pause on the next line for further inspection.

12. Press Command-Option-R to unpause the VM and return control to the VM.

    Let's terminate the debug session and clear any stray breakpoints.

13. While in the IntelliJ editor, press Command-F2 to terminate the debugger.

14. In the top menu, choose Run > View Breakpoints.

15. Click the minus icon to remove all the Dart line breakpoints (**Figure 2.9**).

## DART IN WEBSTORM AND OTHERS

Although IntelliJ IDEA Community Edition is an extremely powerful and free IDE, other solutions are available that might better fit your workflow. These include—but are not limited to—WebStorm, Sublime, Vim, Emacs, and Eclipse. Depending on the level of integration each IDE provides, you might need to download the Dart SDK and Dartium separately.

Google's documentation suggests using WebStorm as the proprietary editor of choice when developing Dart applications. At the time of this writing, the biggest advantage that WebStorm offers over its open-source counterpart, IDEA Community Edition, is support for live browser debugging of Dart code. This enables you to use the same debugger we used for command-line applications, but in a Dartium browser session. If you choose to stick with the open-source setup, you can get similar debugging functionality from Dartium's built-in developer tools.

# OPTIONAL HOMEBREW

Homebrew is a popular package manager for Mac OS X. The Google Dart team has added an official Homebrew tap that enables OS X users with Homebrew installed to download and maintain the most recent stable standalone versions of the Dart SDK and Dartium. You can learn more about homebrew at http://brew.sh.

Once Homebrew is installed, you can use some simple command-line code to maintain your versions:

```
$ brew tap dart-lang/dart
$ brew install dart dartium
$ brew linkapps dart dartium
```

Part of the benefit of using Homebrew's managed instance is that your binaries are automatically exposed to your local environment path.

# SUMMARY

Congratulations—you've run through the basics of executing a Dart application. In this chapter you looked at how to set up basic projects using JetBrains' IntelliJ Community Edition IDE. By doing so, you executed examples of Dart running on the server and Dart running in the browser. You even learned the basics of how to debug Dart in both contexts.

Now that you know the basics about running Dart code, the next few chapters introduce you to many of the structural elements of the Dart language.

## YOU SHOULD KNOW:

- How to acquire the Dart SDK
- How to acquire the Dartium browser
- How to set your environment variables
- How to acquire and install a free open-source IDE from IntelliJ
- How to add support for Dart to IntelliJ
- How to execute a command-line application
- How to execute a browser application in Dartium
- How to execute a browser application in other browsers
- How to debug a Dart console application
- How to debug a Dart web application

# CHAPTER 3

# Introduction to the Dart Language

This chapter includes a series of concise code examples to illustrate many language features found in Dart. You will structure a project for execution as a command-line application. This will allow you to focus solely on the language features. You'll dive into how Dart interacts with the browser later in the book.

# CREATING YOUR FIRST DART PROJECT

**FIGURE 3.1**
Parts of a directory structure

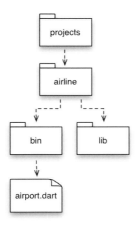

Your first application is going to be for a fictional airline named Just-In-Time Airlines. You're going to manually build out the directory structure to familiarize yourself with the file structure of a Dart project. You'll do an in-depth review of library and directory conventions in Chapter 5.

**NOTE:** IDEA comes with a bunch of great tools for scaffolding large projects, but sometimes you just want a bare-bones application. IDEA actually makes this quite difficult, so we're going to bypass IDEA by manually creating an empty directory and then opening it from inside IDEA.

1. Navigate to your ~/projects folder on your operating system.
2. Create a new folder named `airline`.
3. Open the JetBrains IntelliJ IDEA editor.
4. Click Open on the Welcome screen, or select it from the File menu.
5. In the dialog window, navigate to your ~/projects folder.
6. Highlight the `airline` folder, and click Choose to select it.

   This will import your `airline` project folder into IDEA. Next you'll create some folders inside your `airline` project folder.
7. On the left side of the editor in the IDE's Project panel, Control-click the `airline` folder, and select New > Directory. Name the new directory `bin`.
8. Create another new directory inside your `airline` folder, and name it `lib`.
9. Navigate into the `airline` folder on the left side of the editor. This time create a new file inside your `bin` folder, and name it `airport.dart`.

   The resulting directory structure should look like **Figure 3.1**.

10. Type the following code in the empty `airport.dart` file:

```dart
void main() {
  print('Welcome To Just-In-Time Airlines Terminal Application');
}
```

11. Create a command-line launcher for `airport.dart` using the same approach you learned in Chapter 2 in the section "Command-line Applications."

12. Run the application from inside IDEA. When you run your launcher, you should see the following in your output window:

```
Observatory listening on http://127.0.0.1:52852
Welcome To Just-In-Time Airlines Terminal Application
```

# USING FUNCTIONS IN DART

Functions in Dart are objects with statements that include a set of instructions interpreted by the VM. Functions are the building blocks that compose the core set of logic for your application. In fact, although it's not advised, your entire application could be a single function.

## APPLICATION ENTRY POINT AND MAIN()

The entry-point file provides the initial run-time context for the remainder of the application. All further system activity operates with the entry-point file as the root location. All Dart applications invoke a named function of `main()` to begin a program's execution loop. A Dart entry-point file can be any file that implements `main()`.

In step 10 of the last section, you defined an application entry point by declaring function `main()` in your `airport.dart` file. Let's run it from the command line:

1. Open your operating system terminal application.

2. Navigate to the `airline` folder at `~/projects/airline`.

3. Execute the following code from that folder:

```
$ dart bin/airport.dart
```

You should see the following output:

```
Welcome To Just-In-Time Airlines Terminal Application
```

What you've done so far:

- In `airport.dart`, you declared a function named `main()` and set an optional return type of `void`.

- In `airport.dart`, you called a function named `print()` and passed a string literal as an argument.

- From the command line, you instantiated Dart VM and passed it a root entry point of `airport.dart`.
- By providing a path to the root entry-point file, you instructed Dart VM to execute the `main()` function.

## FUNCTIONS AND OPTIONAL RETURN TYPES

The Dart VM does not expect an object to be returned by the entry point. Therefore, the `main()` function defined in `airport.dart` has a return type of void. This is an optionally typed function. The void type tells the Dart interpreter not to allow the return of an object to the function caller. The void type could be omitted, and the program would continue to function as expected.

1. Modify the `airport.dart` file to match **Example 3.1**, which includes a few examples of different return type declarations.

   **EXAMPLE 3.1**
   ```
   main() {
     print( getWelcomeMessage() );
   }

   String getWelcomeMessage() {
     return 'Welcome To ' + getAirlineName() + ' Terminal Application';
   }

    getAirlineName() {
     return "Just-In-Time";
   }
   ```

   If you execute `airport.dart` again, you'll see the same output string printed. However, after this modification, you've removed the string literal and spread it out over a few different function calls, starting with `getWelcomeMessage()`.

   In Dart, "function" is not a keyword like it is in other C-style languages. Functions look like other fields but with parentheses to accept arguments and curly braces to delineate an execution block.

   In Example 3.1, you defined two new functions. Inside the application's `main()` function, you are executing a `getWelcomeMessage()` function and passing its returned value as an argument to `print()`.

   The `getWelcomeMessage()` function has an assigned return type of `String`. This indicates that the function must return an object, and that object must be of type `String`; otherwise, the Dart analyzer will report an error.

Later in the program, the getAirlineName() function appears to be untyped, because it does not have a class identifier as a prefix. All functions that omit the type are automatically assigned a type of dynamic.

The following function declaration is the same as Example 3.1 except that **Example 3.2** makes explicit the return type of dynamic.

**EXAMPLE 3.2**

```
dynamic getAirlineName() {
  return "Just-In-Time";
}
```

2. Change both of the functions' return values to an int literal of 1 (**Example 3.3**).

**EXAMPLE 3.3**

```
String getWelcomeMessage() {
  return 1;
}


 getAirlineName() {
  return 1;
}
```

Let's take a look at some feedback from the IDEA editor. Make sure the Dart Analysis window is open.

3. In the top menu bar, choose View > Tool Windows > Dart Analysis.

If one is not already open, this will open a new panel at the bottom of the IDE. You'll notice that after making the changes from Example 3.3, there's a warning in the window for the function declaration of getWelcomeMessage reading: The return type 'int' is not a 'String', as defined by the method 'getWelcomeMessage'.

Farther down, notice that the untyped dynamic function has no warnings. A dynamic function accepts any object as a return type; this is dangerous because the calling code expects the function to return a string and cannot handle an integer.

Executing the code in Example 3.3 results in _TypeError at run time. But you should expect that, because the Dart Analysis plugin was giving you immediate feedback about type mismatches.

Let's restore your code to Example 3.1 before moving on. IDEA keeps a linear history of the edits applied to your file.

4. Press Command-Z to walk backward through the history of your edits.

## FIRST-CLASS FUNCTIONS

Dart supports first-class functions. That means you can use functions in the same way you'd use any other object: You can pass a function reference as an argument to a different function, return a function reference as a value from inside a function, or assign a function reference to a variable.

## FUNCTION REFERENCE AND FUNCTION VALUES

You can store a reference to a function in a local variable in the same way you store any object reference. In the following code, you're going to initialize a local variable named aNameGetter of type Function and assign it a reference. By omitting the parentheses, you are assigning the function reference getAirlineName and not the function's returned value.

In **Example 3.4**, when you execute the return statement, aNameGetter() executes the reference to getAirlineName whose function block returns the string value.

**EXAMPLE 3.4**

```
String getWelcomeMessage() {
  Function aNameGetter; //the declared local variable
  aNameGetter = getAirlineName; //the variable assignment
  return 'Welcome To ' + aNameGetter() + ' Terminal Application';
}


String getAirlineName() {
  return "Just-In-Time";
}
```

In **Example 3.5**, you want to acquire a string value and assign it to a variable named name, which will execute the getAirlineName() function and assign its return value upon variable instantiation. The string variable named name is then concatenated in the return statement.

**EXAMPLE 3.5**

```
String getWelcomeMessage() {
  String name = getAirlineName();
  return 'Welcome To ' + name + ' Terminal Application';
}


String getAirlineName() {
  return "Just-In-Time";
}
```

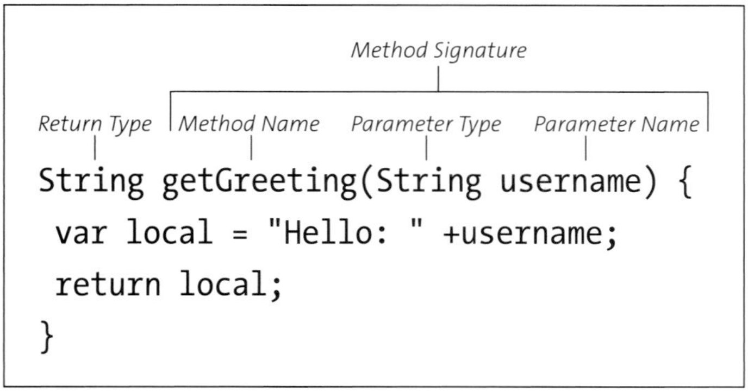

FIGURE 3.2 Parts of a function

## FUNCTION PARAMETERS

The named identifiers inside a function declaration's parentheses are known as parameters, and are collectively referred to as a method signature (**Figure 3.2**). When a function is executed, a calling function can pass in instance references. The instances that are passed into a function on execution are known as arguments.

Dart supports function parameters in a couple of variations. Let's refactor the application to accept the airline name as an argument.

### STANDARD COMMA-DELIMITED PAIRS

The first variation we'll look at is a delimited pair of types and parameter names. In this approach, all values are supplied by the calling expression with objects matching the ordered positions defined in the function declaration (**Example 3.6**).

### EXAMPLE 3.6

```
String getWelcomeMessage(String aName, int aYear) {
  return 'Welcome To ' + aName + ' Terminal Application. Copyright $aYear';
}

void main() {
  String _name = "Just-In-Time";
  int _copyrightYear = 2015;
  print( getWelcomeMessage(_name, _copyrightYear) );
}
```

## POSITIONAL OPTIONAL PARAMETERS AND DEFAULT VALUES

Sometimes you don't want the calling expression to supply all the possible arguments. Dart supports optional arguments with default values.

An optional argument must occur after all required arguments. You can have single or multiple optional arguments, but they must all be wrapped with square brackets [ ] as shown by the code highlight in **Example 3.7**.

**EXAMPLE 3.7**

```
String getWelcomeMessage(String aName, [int aYear=2015,
→ String aMonth='January']) {
 return 'Welcome To ' + aName + ' Terminal Application.
→ Copyright $aMonth $aYear';
}

void main() {
  String _name = "Just-In-Time";
  int _copyrightYear = 1985;
  String _copyrightMonth = "June";
  print( getWelcomeMessage(_name) );
  print( getWelcomeMessage(_name, _copyrightYear) );
  print( getWelcomeMessage(_name, _copyrightYear, _copyrightMonth) );
}

//Output
//Welcome To Just-In-Time Terminal Application. Copyright June 2015
//Welcome To Just-In-Time Terminal Application. Copyright June 1985
//Welcome To Just-In-Time Terminal Application. Copyright February 1985
```

## NAMED PARAMETERS AND DEFAULT VALUES

Named parameters are ideal to use when you have a large set of arguments. Named parameters are not order dependent. Instead, they require a key to match against.

If you have a set of 10 possible arguments, you can pass in only the last item by specifying the argument's name and ignoring the rest. The unspecified arguments will be assigned null.

A named argument must occur after all required arguments. You can have single or multiple named arguments, but they must all be wrapped with brackets { } as in **Example 3.8**.

**EXAMPLE 3.8**

```dart
String getWelcomeMessage({String name, int year:2015, String month:'June'}) {
  if(name == null) {
    name = "--";
  }
  return 'Welcome To ' + name + ' Terminal Application. Copyright $month $year';
}

void main() {
  String _name = "Just-In-Time";
  int _copyrightYear = 1985;
  String _copyrightMonth = "February";
  print( getWelcomeMessage() );
  print( getWelcomeMessage(month: _copyrightMonth) );
  print( getWelcomeMessage(month: _copyrightMonth, name: _name) );
  print( getWelcomeMessage(year: _copyrightYear, month: _copyrightMonth) );
}

//Output
//Welcome To -- Terminal Application. Copyright June 2015
//Welcome To --Terminal Application. Copyright February 2015
//Welcome To Just-In-Time Terminal Application. Copyright February 2015
//Welcome To -- Terminal Application. Copyright February 1985
```

**NOT BOTH**

You can use either named optional parameters or positional optional parameters, but you cannot use both in the same method signature.

## PRIMITIVES

At the time of this writing, Dart has six primitive objects: null, num, bool, double, String, and enum. Primitives in Dart are the most basic elements of a language. They are what more complex objects are built of. They tend to hold one unit of data.

## PRIMITIVES PASSED AS VALUES

When passing primitives as arguments to a function, the expression is interpreted as a value. This affects integers, Booleans, and numbers. In contrast, an object's expression is interpreted as a reference, and the result is a reference being passed into the function.

This means that when you modify an argument that is of a primitive type inside the function's scope, it affects only the variable inside the function's scope.

Conversely, when you modify an object reference inside a function's scope, the referenced object is acted upon and the results are persisted inside the function, in the caller's scope, and in any other place that has a reference to the object. Take a look at **Example 3.9**.

**EXAMPLE 3.9**

```
main() {
  String pilot = "Jack Murphy";
  Map company = { 'airline': "Just-In-Time"};
  passByValues(pilot, company);
  print('-- Check 3');
  print('pilot: ' + pilot); //change lost
  print('map object: ' +  company.toString() );  //change persisted
}


void passByValues(String name, Map vo) {
  print('-- Check 1');
  print('name: ' + name);
  print('value object: ' +  vo.toString() );
  name = "Amelia Earhart"; //modify a primitive
  vo['airline'] = "TWA"; //modify an object
  print('-- Check 2');
  print('name: ' + name);
  print('value object: ' +  vo.toString() );
}


//Output:
//-- Check 1
//name: Jack Murphy
//value object: {airline: Just-In-Time}
//-- Check 2
//name: Amelia Earhart
//value object: {airline: TWA}
//-- Check 3
//pilot: Jack Murphy
//map object: {airline: TWA}
```

The code passes in a primitive string named pilot, and a map named company in function passByValues(). Map is a composite object made up of multiple objects. Because Map is not a primitive, its expression evaluates to an object reference. Inside the function, you modify both argument instances. Since you've marked the return type as void, there is no returned object.

Back in the calling function at Check 3, you see that only one of the two changes persisted. The change on the map persisted because the expression company is interpreted as a reference when passed into the function as vo. The reference maintains the relationship to the company variable in the caller's scope.

The primitive string value did not persist in the caller because the string expression for pilot is interpreted as a value, and therefore loses any relationship to the caller. The string identifier named name inside the passByValues() function becomes a unique instance scoped only to that function.

# DART OBJECTS AND MAPS

All of Dart's classes are descendants of the class Object. The Object class has a very sparse interface consisting of only a handful of methods implementing base-level functionality, including toString(), noSuchMethod(), hashCode, and runtimeType.

The workhorse of the Dart language is the map object. A map is a key-value pair object implementation that is a direct descendent of class Object. Maps can be created inline using map literals with curly bracket notation, or by using the new constructor on the Map class.

```
Map company = { 'airline': 'Just-In-Time', 'city': 'San Francisco'};
```

   Or

```
Map company = new Map();
company['airline'] = 'Just-In-Time';
company['city'] = 'San Francisco';
```

## ACCESSING PROPERTIES OF A MAP

To access a property on a map instance, an argument must be supplied using square bracket notation, such as object['key'], as in **Example 3.10**. A key can be a string literal, or an object reference. If you're coming from JavaScript, be aware that you cannot use a dot operator to access the property's value.

**EXAMPLE 3.10**
```
main() {
Map company = new Map();
company['airline'] = 'Just-In-Time';
company['city'] = 'San Francisco';

print( company['city'] ); //prints San Francisco
print( company['airline'] ); //prints Just-In-Time
print( company['non-existent'] ); //prints null
}
```

## DETERMINING OBJECT EQUALITY

Dart has two approaches to determine if two references are the same: the == operator and the top-level function identical. The == operator has a default implementation in class Object that implements the identical() function. An Object subclass can override its == operator for cases such as collection value matching. In the default implementation, the identical() function returns a Boolean of true if the references match.

The num class has its own implementation of the == operator to support comparisons between doubles and integers. The default num equality functionality converts a double to an int and then compares the values. If the double that is being compared to an int is a fractional value, it returns a false value because ints do not have the precision to be a match. **Example 3.11** shows examples of equality statements and how they evaluate.

**EXAMPLE 3.11**

```dart
main() {

  Map company = { 'airline': "Just-In-Time", 'city': 'San Francisco'};
  Map duplicate = { 'airline': "Just-In-Time", 'city': 'San Francisco'};
  Map expression = company; //shared reference

  String answer;

  answer = identical(company, company).toString();
  print("is company identical to company: " + answer ); //true

  answer = identical(company, expression).toString();
  print("is company identical to expression: " + answer ); //true

  answer = identical(company, duplicate).toString();
  print("is company identical to duplicate: " + answer ); //false

  answer = (company == duplicate).toString();
  print("is company == to duplicate: " + answer ); //false

  answer = (company == expression).toString();
  print("is company == to expression: " + answer ); //true

  answer = (5.0 == 5).toString();
  print( "is double 5.0 == int 5: " + answer); //true
```

```
  answer = (5.5 == 5).toString();
  print( "is double 5.5 == int 5: " + answer ); //false


  answer = (5 == 5).toString();
  print( "is int 5 == int 5: " + answer ); //true


  answer = identical(5.0, 5.0).toString();
  print("is double 5.0 identical to double 5.0: " + answer ); //true


  answer = identical(5.0, 5).toString();
  print( "is double 5.0 identical to int 5: " + answer ); //false


  answer = identical(5.5, 5).toString();
  print("is double 5.5 identical to int 5: " + answer ); //false


  answer = identical(5, 5).toString();
  print("is int 5 identical to int 5: " + answer); //true
}
```

# STATEMENTS AND CONTROL STRUCTURES

Dart uses the traditional parentheses and curly braces for flow control. Dart's control structures should look familiar to anyone with a background using a C-style language.

## CONDITIONALS WITH IF-THEN-ELSE

Dart is very strict about what qualifies as an acceptable valid condition. Dart allows only a Boolean object of value true to execute an if statement. Empty strings are not a match, an empty but instantiated object is not a match, and no number qualifies as a match. Only a Boolean of value true will be allowed to execute a positive if statement.

```
if(true) {
  print("This is true");
} else if("") {
  print("This is will never get called");
} else {
  print("This would execute of true was false");
}
```

## ITERATION USING FOR LOOPS

Dart has a traditional for loop that accepts three arguments: an initialization expression, a termination expression, and an increment expression. The following example will print an index range starting from 0 and terminate after a printing an index value of 9.

```
for(var index = 0; index < 10; index++)
{
  print("iteration index of: $index");
}
```

Dart also supports a for-in loop that is ideal for iterating over a typed collection. The following example iterates over a typed list of strings. You can optionally use the dynamic type var if your list contains multiple types of values.

```
List<String> words = ['eeny', 'meeni', 'mini', mo'];
for(String item in words) {
  print(item);
}
```

The next example iterates over all the keys in a Map object and prints out the corresponding key-value pair.

```
Map company = {'airline': "Just-In-Time", 'city': 'San Francisco'};
for(String key in company.keys){
  print('key: ' + key);
  print('value: ' + company[key]);
}
```

## WHILE LOOPS

A while loop executes a statement as long as the condition is a Boolean value of true. Again, Dart is very strict about what constitutes true. The following condition uses a traditional loop to execute only once.

```
bool aToggle = true;
while(aToggle)
{
  aToggle = false
}
```

If the aToggle value was false, the statement will execute 0 times. If you want to ensure that your statement always executes at least once, you can use a do-while loop.

```dart
do {
  print("I execute a minimum of once time")
}
while(false);
```

## CONTROLLING LOOPS

Dart supports break and continue when executing inside of iterators, such as for-loops, while-loops, or switch-cases.

Using the continue keyword causes the current iteration to finish and move to the next iteration.

Using the break keyword terminates the loop execution regardless of the value of the Boolean value in the conditional check (**Example 3.12**).

**EXAMPLE 3.12**

```dart
main() {
  num index = 0;
  while(true) {
    print(index);
    if(index == 10)
    {
      //set the value and then skip to the next iteration
      index = 20;
      continue;
    } else if(index == 20) {
      //This executes on the next iteration.
      //You cant change the literal bool of true in the while condition,
      //but this loop terminates because of break.
      break;
    }
    index++;
  }
}
```

## SWITCH AND CASE

Dart has support for switch and case statements, which are used for controlling flow based on a single matching expression against multiple possible values. Dart is strict about each case keyword being paired with a closing break keyword. The exception to this rule is for grouping multiple cases into one executable statement. Switch statements also work well with Dart's support for enums (**Example 3.13**).

**EXAMPLE 3.13**

```dart
enum Airports {SFO, LAX, DAL, HOU}

main() {
  Airports city = Airports.SFO;

  switch(city) {
  case Airports.SFO:
    print('we found SFO'); //this prints
    break;
  case Airports.LAX:
    print('we could find LAX');
    break;
  case Airports.DAL:
  case Airports.HOU:
    print('we could find a group of airports in texas');
    break;
  default:
    print("We didn't find any airports");
  }

}
```

# ERRORS ON ASSERT()

Dart has a built-in assert method when running in checked mode. Dart bypasses all assert methods when your code is pushed to production. This is great for run-time checks while developing, or for writing unit tests.

Dart's assert() method is used for checking an argument that is passed in as a Boolean value. If it's true, the program execution continues uninterrupted. If it's anything other than a Boolean true, an AssertionError will be thrown and the program execution will terminate.

```
int anInteger = 1;
assert(1 == 1); //This assertion passes
assert(anInteger); //This assertion fails and program execution halts
```

# COLLECTIONS AND ITERATORS

Understanding and efficiently working with collections and iterators is an integral part of an engineer's job, and it's important that the chosen language supports that role with concise, performant options for the many use cases for dealing with large collections of data. Luckily, Dart has great language support for working with collections. Let's take a look at what's available.

Instead of an array class of objects, Dart collections share a superclass named Iterable. Iterable is an interface that allows an iterator to serve up an object from a collection one at a time. There are many classes that implement Iterable, but the most commonly used are List, Queue, and Set.

## LIST

A list in Dart is, by default, an expandable collection of objects that you can modify via a zero-based index location. It can be instantiated with the List literal syntax of square brackets, or with the new List() constructor. The constructor takes an optional parameter of type int if the author would like to create a fixed-length list.

```
List words = new List(5); //empty fixed length list of type generic
List mixed = ['Fuel', 1, 'Wheel', 2]; //list literal
```

The default state of a list is to accept elements of type generic, otherwise known as untyped. This means you can add an int, num, double, or String object to the same list. However, if you want a list to accept only a certain type, you can specify that at the time of declaration using the diamond syntax <Class>, as seen in the following:

```
List<String> snacks = new List<String>();  //empty growable list of type String
snacks.add("Nuts");
snacks.add("Soda");
snacks.add("Coffee");
snacks.add("Crackers");
snacks.add(1); //throws _TypeError: 'int' is not a subtype of type 'String'
```

The List class has a large number of built-in helper methods that are extremely useful. I could fill a couple of chapters just looking at the List API. I highly suggest checking out the docs for more information.

## QUEUE

A queue in Dart is, by default, an expandable collection of objects (**Example 3.14**) that is optimized to be modified or accessed from either the beginning or end of the collection. Unlike List, Queue has no index access.

**NOTE:** Chapter 5 covers the *import* keyword.

**EXAMPLE 3.14**
```
import 'dart:collection';
main() {
  Queue gates = new Queue();
  gates.addFirst('C');
  gates.addFirst('B');
  gates.addFirst('A');
  var rItem = gates.removeFirst();
  gates.addLast('D');
  gates.addLast('E');
  gates.addLast('E');
  gates.addLast('E');
  gates.addLast('F');
  gates.removeLast();
```

```
  print(gates);
  print('rItem: ' + rItem);
}

//Output:
//{B, C, D, E, E, E}
//rItem: A
```

## SET

A set in Dart is, by default, an expandable collection of objects that ensures uniqueness of the objects in its collection of elements. Starting with an empty set and then attempting to add the same element multiple times will still result in a set with a length of 1. A set does not ensure order the way a collection or queue does.

```
Set years = new Set();
years.add(1997);
years.add(1997);
years.add(1997);
print("Set Length: " + years.length.toString() );

//Output:
//Set Length: 1
```

# NUMBERS

Dart ships with two numeric data types. Both types are decendents of type num. Dart handles numeric values differently than some other C-style languages. num, and its descendants, int and double, share a superclass of type Object.

To ensure performant behavior, Dart uses a process called *unboxing,* which allows numeric values to sit inside the CPU register instead of adding to the memory stack. This allows numeric operations to result in a new object without incurring high performance costs.

## INT

Dart has an arbitrarily sized integer. When converted to JavaScript, int has a cap of 53 bits. When running server side through the Dart VM, an int is made up of three internal representations that scale on demand to support the required level of precision. These are smi, mint, and bigint. The final size limitation of int's type bigint is the system RAM.

```
int anIndex = 1; //this is ok
anIndex = 1.19 //Error type 'double' is not a subtype of type 'int'
```

## DOUBLE

Doubles are floating point values that adhere to the IEEE 754 standard.

```
double pi = 3.141592653589793; //accurate to 15 slots
print(pi);
double imprecise = 3.14159265358979323846;
print(imprecise); //truncated to 15 slots- loses precision from original value
```

## TYPED NUMERIC LIST

When storing collections, Dart has a large library of typed collection classes. These are located in the dart:typed_data package.

You can select from classes such as Int8List, Int32List, Int64List, Float32List, and so on. Typed lists can be run more efficiently because the Dart VM has enough information, based on the selected type and list length, to make more compact collections in memory (**Example 3.15**).

**EXAMPLE 3.15**
```
import 'dart:typed_data';
main() {
//defines list length to allocate correct amount of memory
Float64List dollars = new Float64List(4);
  dollars[0] = 1.0;
  dollars[1] = 2.0;
  dollars[2] = 1; //Error 'int' is not a subtype of type 'double' of 'value'
}
```

This code accesses the locations by index since you cannot add elements to a fixed-length list.

**NOTE:** Since JavaScript doesn't support typed_data, and all numbers are represented as doubles, some of the performance gains in Dart VM might degrade when running in a JavaScript VM.

## ENUMS

Enums help with legibility while working with multiple fixed values. An enum is an object that allows you to associate multiple fixed constant named values with a data type.

The named value is automatically assigned a corresponding index value based on the order in which it was defined. If used, an enum must be instantiated at the class level (**Example 3.16**).

**EXAMPLE 3.16**

```
enum Airports {SFO, LAX, DAL}

main() {
  print(Airports.LAX); //Airports.LAX
  print(Airports.LAX.index); //1 is the index value of LAX
  print(Airports.SFO); //Airports.SFO
  print(Airports.SFO.index); //0 is the index value OF SFO
  print(Airports.values); //[Airports.SFO, Airports.LAX, Airports.DAL]
}
```

## EXCEPTIONS

Exceptions are Error events that are added to the call stack and that, if allowed to bubble to the top, terminate program execution. When added to the stack, the current stack trace is appended to the object to assist with debugging. Exceptions can be handled using the try-catch syntax, or emitted using the top-level throw method.

The code in **Example 3.17** executes a try-catch statement and intentionally throws an error:

**EXAMPLE 3.17**

```
main() {
  try {
    print("Try and take off backwards... ");
    throw new Error();
  } catch(exception, stackTrace) {
    print("Exception is: " + exception.toString() );
    print(stackTrace);
  }
  print("End of Function");
}
```

```
//Output:
//Try and take off backwards...
//Exception is: Instance of 'Error'
//#0      main
→ (file:///Users/jmurphy/projects/dart_console_temp/bin/main.dart:16:5)
//#1      _startIsolate.<anonymous closure>
→ (dart:isolate-patch/isolate_patch.dart:255)
//#2      _RawReceivePortImpl._handleMessage
→ (dart:isolate-patch/isolate_patch.dart:142)
//End of Function
```

As you can see, you get a helpful stack trace with the function and the file location that the exception originated in. You also get an instance of the Error class that was thrown.

Although an exception was raised, it was handled by the try-catch statement, so program execution continued outside the try-catch block. It's best to use try-catch blocks sparingly, because they can disguise severe problems with your application.

The implementation in Example 3.17 will catch all errors within the default scope of the try-catch statement. You can make a catch type specific by using the on Type declaration (**Example 3.18**). This will ignore all other error types.

**EXAMPLE 3.18**

```
main() {
  try {
    print("Do Thing... Uh Oh...");
    throw new CastError();
  } on CastError catch(exception, stackTrace) {
    print("CastError caught...");
  } catch(exception, stackTrace) {
    print("All other errors caught...");
  }
}


//Output:
//Do Thing... Uh Oh...
//CastError caught...
```

# SUMMARY

This chapter looked at many of the core classes and concepts that make up the foundation of the Dart language. By mastering these, you'll have a solid capacity to begin solving problems in Dart.

The next few chapters allow you to use the skills learned here to build reusable classes and, eventually, libraries that can be published publicly for widespread use.

## YOU SHOULD KNOW:

- How to define and execute an application entry point
- How to define and write a function
- How to define and write a return type
- How to request parameters and pass arguments
- The ramifications of using a value instead of an object as an argument passed into a function
- How to instantiate and access properties of numeric types, maps, enums, and lists
- How to control the flow of execution through conditional blocks and over collections
- How to raise an error when needed

**CHAPTER 4**

# Object Structures in Dart

One of the most attractive Dart enhancements is the ability to craft proper object taxonomies using object-oriented principles, such as inheritance and traditional design patterns. Dart offers many language features to help encapsulate code while making it easy to reuse behaviors, classes, and libraries. This chapter introduces you to the language features, and Chapter 5 looks at how to leverage these features by focusing on how Dart structures objects and their corresponding object scopes.

# VARIABLES

A *variable* is a named identifier accessible from within the current scope. Variables, depending on the object type, can store a reference to either a value or an object instance. Dart supports first-class functions, so variables can also store references to functions.

A variable statement in Dart consists of a type annotation, a unique named identifier, and an optional assignment. Dart supports the keyword var, which is shorthand to register the variable instance with an assigned type of dynamic.

In the following approach, you're going to initialize a variable named company of type dynamic within the scope of the main() function.

```
main() {
  var company = {'publisher': "Peachpit"};
}
```

The code runs, but by using var, any developer could come along and assign a string or a number to the variable. If you use Dart's support for type annotations, you can ensure that any reference that is assigned to company is of type Map.

```
main() {
  Map company = { 'publisher': "Peachpit"};
}
```

You cannot completely omit the type declaration or Dart will assume it's an assignment to a previously declared variable, attempt to look up the name from within the current scope, and fail to find it.

```
main() {
  company = { 'publisher': "Peachpit"}; //throws method not found: 'company='
}
```

**NOTE:** Unlike similar languages, Dart does not support variable hoisting. Variable hoisting is the process of allowing variables that are declared later in the execution context of the same scope to resolve prior to actual declaration. In Dart, you must declare a variable prior to attempting to access it.

# LEXICAL SCOPE

Scope delineates the reach of an inferred namespace where you can directly access named identifiers. Scope, in Dart, is delineated by each new set of curly braces. Each set of curly braces acquires its own new scope while inheriting from the scope in which it was declared.

Dart is a lexically scoped language. With lexical scoping, descendant scopes will access the most recently declared variable of the same name. The innermost scope is searched first, followed by a search outward through other enclosing scopes.

```
{
  //search outermost last
  String name = "Jack Murphy"
  {
    //search innermost first
    print(name)
  }
}
```

Let's define a nested function inside main(). Inside the inner() function, declare two variables named **level** and **example**. These variables will be available *only* inside the wrapping scope (**Example 4.1**).

**EXAMPLE 4.1**

```
main() {
  void inner ()
  {
      int level = 1; //not visible in main()
      String example = "scope"; //not visible in main()
      print('example: $example, level: $level');
  }
  inner(); //calls the function which prints - example: scope, level: 1
}
```

Let's try to access the variables of example and level outside the inner() function.

**EXAMPLE 4.2**

```
main() {
  void inner()
  {
    int level = 1;
    String example = "scope";
    print('example: $example, level: $level');
  }
  inner();
  print('level: $level and example: $example'); //results in an Error
}
```

In the Dart Analyzer, you'll see that the `print()` line in **Example 4.2** results in an error: `undefined name 'level'`. Let's take a look at how a scope inherits from the scope in which it's declared and how it searches for named identifiers from inside out.

**EXAMPLE 4.3**

```
main() { //a new scope
  String language = "Dart";

  void outer()  {
    //curly bracket opens a child scope with inherited variables

    String level = 'one';
    String example = "scope";

    void inner() { //another child scope with inherited variables
      //the next 'level' variable has priority over previous
      //named variable in the outer scope with the same named identifier
      Map level = {'count': "Two"};
      //prints example: scope, level:two
      print('example: $example, level: $level');
      //inherited from the outermost scope: main
      print('What Language: $language');
    } //end inner scope

    inner();

    //prints example: scope, level:one
    print('example: $example, level: $level');
  } //end outer scope
  outer();
} //end main scope
```

In **Example 4.3**, `inner()` inherits scope from `outer()`, which inherits scope from `main()`. This gives `inner()` access to the outermost scope where the variable `language` is accessible. Conversely, `main()` has no idea of the existence of function `inner()`.

To further illustrate lexical scope, let's take a look at the hashcode property of each variable from within its respective scope.

A *hashcode* is a value generated by converting each property of an object to a numeric value and then joining those values together to create a single numeric representation of the entire object. Hashcodes are not guaranteed to be the same between runs or on different machines. Objects of differing values or differing types cannot share the same hashcode. Hashcodes give us a uniform approach to compare variables, as shown in **Example 4.4**.

**EXAMPLE 4.4**

```
main() {
  String language = "Dart";
  void outer()  {
    String level = 'one';
    String example = "scope";

    void inner() {
      //declare a new variable named level in memory on the 'inner' scope
      //even though the named identifier is the same as the variable in outer()
      Map level = {'count': "Two"};

      print('-----');
      print('inner::outer.hashcode ' + outer.hashCode.toString());
      print('inner::inner.hashcode ' + outer.hashCode.toString());
      print('inner::language.hashcode ' + language.hashCode.toString());
      print('inner::example.hashcode ' + example.hashCode.toString());
      print('inner::level.hashcode ' + level.hashCode.toString());
    }
    //has access to only outer scope variables
    print('-----');
    print('outer::outer.hashcode ' + outer.hashCode.toString());
    print('outer::inner.hashcode ' + outer.hashCode.toString());
    print('outer::language.hashcode ' + language.hashCode.toString());
    print('outer::example.hashcode ' + example.hashCode.toString());
    print('outer::level.hashcode ' + level.hashCode.toString());
    inner();
  }
  print('-----');
  print('main::language.hashcode ' + language.hashCode.toString());
  print('main::outer.hashcode ' + outer.hashCode.toString());
  print('main::inner.hashcode N/A');
```

```
    outer();
}

//Output:
//main::language.hashcode 482586172
//main::outer.hashcode 380883474
//main::inner.hashcode N/A
//-----
//outer::outer.hashcode 380883474
//outer::inner.hashcode 380883474
//outer::language.hashcode 482586172
//outer::example.hashcode 857747343
//outer::level.hashcode 1058535322
//-----
//inner::outer.hashcode 380883474
//inner::inner.hashcode 380883474
//inner::language.hashcode 482586172
//inner::example.hashcode 857747343
//inner::level.hashcode 802594681
```

**Table 4.1** is a matrix of hashcodes for each object from within its respective scopes.

The empty cells in Table 4.1 illustrate that objects that are declared only inside a child scope, such as `outer()`, are not accessible from parent scopes, such as `main()`.

As you can see in Table 4.1, `inner()` inherits scope from `outer()` but also declares its own named identifier of the variable `level`.

The second declaration of `level` as a `Map` does not modify the variable in scope `outer()`, but instead creates a new variable with its own object reference that's *only* accessible within the scope for `inner()`. After the new `level` variable is initialized within scope `inner()`, the hashcode for the variable `level` inside the scope of `inner()` reports as 802594681 instead of 1058535322.

**TABLE 4.1** Example Object Hashcode Matrix

| OBJECT | SCOPE: main{ } | SCOPE: outer{ } | SCOPE: inner{ } |
|---|---|---|---|
| outer | 380883474 | 380883474 | 380883474 |
| language | 482586172 | 482586172 | 482586172 |
| inner | | 380883474 | 380883474 |
| level | | 1058535322 | 802594681 |
| example | | 857747343 | 857747343 |

# CLASSES

Classes expose functionality on how to construct a new instance of a requested object type, functionality to expose methods and data, and functionality that encapsulates variables to track object state within its scope.

Every object in Dart is an instance of a class. You've been using Dart's built-in classes throughout this book. Some built-in classes that you've worked with so far are Map, String, and List.

## CUSTOM CLASSES

Dart supports single inheritance, meaning that if no superclass is defined, the superclass will default to class Object. Classes allow you to construct your own objects in a declarative fashion. Let's create your first class:

**EXAMPLE 4.5**

```
class Airplane
{
  String color = "Silver";
  String wing = "Triangle";
  int seatCount = 2;
  double fuel = 100.50;
}

main() {
  Airplane yourPlane = new Airplane();
  Airplane myPlane = new Airplane();

  print(myPlane.wing); //prints " Triangle "
  print(myPlane.seatCount); //prints "2"

  yourPlane.seatCount = 1;
  print(yourPlane.seatCount); //prints "1"
}
```

**Example 4.5** accomplished two things. First it defined a class named Airplane with some public fields. Next, in the main() function, it instantiated two new object instances of class type Airplane named yourPlane and myPlane.

Upon instantiation, the field values of color, fuel, seatCount, and wing for both yourPlane and myPlane have matching field values. This is because their field values are assigned default values, and both are created from the class Airplane.

The Airplane class exposes seatCount as a public integer, so you are able to modify the seatCount value by using dot notation to access yourPlane.seatCount. All public class fields can be accessed using the dot syntax.

Why did you modify the seatCount? Well, to make the plane lighter of course! Let's add a method that will return the weight of the plane (**Example 4.6**).

**EXAMPLE 4.6**

```
class Airplane
{
  String primaryColor = "Silver";
  String wing = "Triangle";
  int seatCount = 2;
  double fuelCapacity = 100.50;

  double getWeight() {
    return 1000 + seatCount + fuelCapacity;
  }
}

main() {
  Airplane yourPlane = new Airplane();
  Airplane myPlane = new Airplane();
  yourPlane.seatCount = 1;
  print( 'yourplane weight:'+ yourPlane.getWeight().toString() );
  print( 'myplane weight: '+ myPlane.getWeight().toString() );
}
//Output:
//yourplane weight: 1101.5
//myplane weight: 1102.5
```

## INFERRED NAMESPACE

Namespaces are *not* a language feature in Dart, but the concept exists. A *namespace* is an area in your program where a named identifier can be called with only the unique name, and no prefix, to access an object. Conceptually, in Dart, a namespace is the sum of all the inherited scopes.

The "Lexical Scope" section talked about how curly brackets delineate scope hierarchies. The combined output of these inherited scopes creates the active namespace.

If you look at the class statement, you'll notice that all the Airplane fields are wrapped inside a new class scope named Airplane.

```
class Airplane
{
    //declaration
    //declaration
    //declaration
    //declaration
}
```

When you instantiate a new class, you create a new instance of the superclass Object, and declare additional class fields by wrapping them in the class's top-level scope. The new fields are directly accessible by their named identifiers within the namespace of the class instance.

The caller in Example 4.6, main(), instantiates a new class instance and assigns it to local variable yourPlane. The variable's named identifier has access to all the fields in the namespace of class Airplane. The main() function calls the print() function with an argument that calls yourPlane.getWeight(). When getWeight() executes, its function block is operating within the namespace delineated by class Airplane.

```
class Airplane
{
    ...
    ...
  double getWeight() {
  // inherits Airplane class scope and appends
  // its new local function scope
  }
}
```

In Chapter 5, you will see how to use libraries to control namespaces using the keywords show, hide, as, part, and part of.

## CLASS CONSTRUCTORS

Constructors allow you to define a method signature with the required arguments to instantiate a new object of a specific type.

Dart has support for "zero argument constructors." You may have noticed that Example 4.5 didn't define a constructor method, or a superclass. Let's modify the Airplane class (as shown in **Example 4.7**) to be a bit more customizable upon instantiation:

**EXAMPLE 4.7**

```
class Airplane
{
  static const double bodyWeight = 1000.00;
  static const double fuelCapacity = 100.50;

  String color;
  String wing;
  int seatCount;

  Airplane(int seatCount, String color, String wing) {
    this.seatCount = seatCount;
    this.color  = color;
    this.wing = wing;
  }

  double getWeight() {
    return bodyWeight + seatCount + fuelCapacity;
  }
}

main() { //new scope
  Airplane yourPlane = new Airplane(1, "White", "Fixed");
  Airplane myPlane = new Airplane(2, "Gold", "Triangle");
  print( 'yourplane weight:'+ yourPlane.getWeight().toString() );
  print( 'myplane weight: '+ myPlane.getWeight().toString() );
}

//Output:
//yourplane weight: 1101.5
//myplane weight: 1102.5
```

## GENERATIVE CONSTRUCTOR

Example 4.7 appended a named `Airplane` constructor function that accepts three arguments using standard comma-delimited parameters. The `Airplane()` constructor function matches the name of the `Airplane` class. This is referred to as a *generative constructor*. The hardcoded values for `color`, `wing`, or `seatCount` are gone. Instead of hardcoded values, the constructor requires that the class fields be assigned by the arguments that are passed in upon instantiation.

## AUTOMATIC CLASS MEMBER VARIABLE INITIALIZATION

If you'll notice, it's not very DRY (Don't Repeat Yourself) to have objects passed into the constructor and then immediately assign them to class fields. If you're going to automatically assign an argument value to a class field, Dart encourages you to use the keyword this inside the method signature. You can refactor the constructor as shown in **Example 4.8**.

**EXAMPLE 4.8**

```dart
class Airplane
{
  static const double bodyWeight = 1000.00;
  static const double fuelCapacity = 100.50;

  String color;
  String wing;
  int seatCount;

  Airplane(int this.seatCount, String this.color, String this.wing) {
    // You can leave off the { } altogether
    // This whole block becomes optional
  }

  double getWeight() {
    return bodyWeight + seatCount + fuelCapacity;
  }
}

main() { //new scope
  Airplane yourPlane = new Airplane(1, "White", "Fixed");
  Airplane myPlane = new Airplane(2, "Gold", "Triangle");
  print( 'yourplane weight:'+ yourPlane.getWeight().toString() );
  print( 'myplane weight: '+ myPlane.getWeight().toString() );
}

//Output:
//yourplane weight: 1101.5
//myplane weight: 1102.5
```

## NAMED CONSTRUCTORS

Named constructors replace the practice of default overriding and offer multiple ways to initialize the same class of object.

Example 4.8 created an Airplane object that is initialized with three optional fields. Let's say you have a different, recurring use case that always has the same wing type and color, but requires a changing seat value. You have older dependencies that require the previous implementation, so let's add a named constructor for the specific type of Airplane as follows:

**EXAMPLE 4.9**

```
class Airplane
{
  static const double bodyWeight = 1000.00;
  static const double fuelCapacity = 100.50;

  String color;
  String wing;
  int seatCount;

  Airplane(int this.seatCount, String this.color, String this.wing);

  Airplane.sparrow(int this.seatCount){
    wing = "Swept";
    color = "Gold";
  }

  Airplane.robin(String this.color){
    seatCount = 1;
    wing = "Swept";
  }

  double getWeight() {
    return bodyWeight + seatCount + fuelCapacity;
  }
}

main() { //new scope
  Airplane yourPlane = new Airplane(1, "White", "Fixed");
  Airplane myPlane = new Airplane(2, "Gold", "Triangle");
```

```
  Airplane brothersPlane = new Airplane.sparrow(10);
  Airplane sistersPlane = new Airplane.robin('red');

  print( 'yourplane weight:'+ yourPlane.getWeight().toString() );
  print( 'myplane weight: '+ myPlane.getWeight().toString() );

  print( 'brothersPlane weight: '+ brothersPlane.getWeight().toString() );
  print( 'sistersPlane color: '+ sistersPlane.color );
}

//Output:
//yourplane weight:1101.5
//myplane weight: 1102.5
//brothersPlane weight: 1110.5
//sistersPlane color: Red
```

Example 4.9 adds a named constructor of `Airplane.sparrow` to the class. It's using *automatic initialization* to assign the `this.seatCount` parameter. The constructor's function block has hardcoded assignments for the class's fields.

`main()` then instantiates a local variable named `brothersPlane` by leveraging the named constructor `sparrow` and the `new` keyword. All `Airplane` instances returned by `Airplane.sparrow` will have swept wings and a color of gold. The only argument accepted by the named constructor `sparrow` is a numeric value to increase the seat count.

A similar pattern is repeated for the named constructor `robin` and the variable instance `sistersPlane`. But in the case of `robin`, the constructor handles building single-seat airplanes of varying colors.

## FACTORY CONSTRUCTORS

To understand a factory constructor, it's important to understand that when a generative constructor is invoked, a new object instance is created in memory. For performance reasons, this can be a bad approach to acquiring objects. A common pattern to enforce object reuse is the pooling pattern.

In a pooling implementation, instead of creating a new object in memory on every request, the pattern requires a small group of objects to be created at run time. When a new pool member object is needed, it's retrieved from the pool. Then, instead of destroying each instance, the unused object is returned to the pool for later reuse.

Factory constructor functions allow you to bypass the default object instantiation process and return an object instance in some other way. You could return an object from memory or use a different approach to initialization. Factories are intentionally flexible.

Factories offload object creation into the factory function's statement while allowing the signature of the instantiator to use the familiar new `NameOfClass()` syntax. Let's compare using a generative constructor against a factory constructor for class `Pool()`:

```
class Pool
{
   Pool() {
   //do nothing for the generative constructor
   //results in a new object instance
  }
}


main() {
  Pool aPool = new Pool();
  print('aPool: ' + aPool.toString() ); //aPool: Instance of 'Pool'
}
```

Prefixing the existing constructor declaration with the keyword of `factory` will show the power of the factory pattern. With a `factory` constructor in place, you bypass object creation. Let's take a look:

```
class Pool
{
   factory Pool() {
    //do nothing in the factory constructor - you'd usually return something
  }
}
```

Note that the calling implementation does not change, but instead of an instance, you get `null`:

```
main() {
  Pool aPool = new Pool();
  print('aPool: ' + aPool.toString() ); //aPool: null
}
```

Let's rig up a fake Pool implementation. For the sake of brevity, this pool will always return a new Pool instance:

```
class Pool
{
  factory Pool() {
    //a pool usually checks for previously constructed objects in cache
    //if we had a cached item, we'd return it, but instead, for brevity,
```

```
  //we'll build a new one using a named constructor
  return new Pool.NamedPoolConstructor();
}


Pool.NamedPoolConstructor();
}
```

This will result in an instance of Pool in main(). It uses the named constructor function-ality from earlier to return a new instance.

Regardless of what the constructor statement actually looks like, factory constructors and generative constructors provide a consistent interface for acquiring an object using the new NameOfClass() syntax.

## STATIC VARIABLES

A static variable is an object that exists on the class definition and not on the object instance. If your current scope has a class in the namespace, you can access the static variable on the class. The value of the static variable can be modified (**Example 4.10**).

**EXAMPLE 4.10**
```
class Tool
{
  static List collection = ['wrench', 'saw', 'hammer'];
}

main() {
  Tool.collection.add('socket');

  Tool.collection.forEach( (String item){
    print('Collection Has A: $item');
  } );
}


// Output:
// Collection Has A: wrench
// Collection Has A: saw
// Collection Has A: hammer
// Collection Has A: socket
```

Rather than instantiate an instance of Tool, you simply access the static variable associated with the class Tool.

## FINAL VARIABLES

A *final variable* can receive only a single run-time assignment. Its assignment must occur upon declaration if being assigned at run time. Once a value is assigned, it cannot be changed. If it's a primitive value, the primitive value is, in practice, immutable. If it's an object like a List, the variable's reference cannot be changed, but the referenced object's fields are mutable. Final variables can also be declared as static like any other variable.

**EXAMPLE 4.11**

```
class Runway
{
  final String item = "Asphalt";
  final List materials = ["Asphalt", "Gravel", "Cement"];
}

main() {
  Runway rw = new Runway();

  //primitives
  print(rw.item); //prints Asphalt
  rw.item = "Concrete"; //Error 'item' cannot be used as a setter, its final

  //object
  rw.materials.add('Sand'); //adds 'Sand' to the List and modifies its value
  rw.materials = ['Steel']; //Error 'Runway' has no instance setter...
}
```

In **Example 4.11**, you can access the value of String item, but you cannot change the reference of String item to a different string, because that would be a second assignment.

You can add() another object to List materials, or use any of its instance methods, as long as you do not assign a new reference to the final variable. The assignment of a List literal to the final variable encounters the same restriction as in the string example: no secondary assignments allowed.

# CONSTANTS

The Dart language supports the const keyword, which results in values or identifiers that are derived and assigned at compile time. The values are then immutable. A const differs from a final in that finals are assigned at run time.

## CONSTANT OBJECTS

Dart supports the keyword const for object instantiation. If an object is declared as being instantiated via the const keyword, it's assigned a value at compile time.

A constant is an instance that is initialized with one of the following:

- A value of a primitive type
- A literal value derived by using only basic or bitwise operators
- A constant constructor

A const does not have access to any run-time values or helper functions to derive its value.

## CONSTANT IDENTIFIERS

Dart supports the keyword const for identifiers. A const identifier is a marked identifier that is assigned a constant object at compile time. It differs from a variable in that it is a named identifier, but its assigned value also cannot be changed.

**EXAMPLE 4.12**

```
main() {
  const double radar_latitude =  40.7834390;  //primitive double
  const double radar_longitude = -73.9773670;  //primitive double
  const List radar_modes = const ['slow', 'medium', 'fast'];  //const object

  print( radar_latitude );
  print( radar_longitude );
  print( radar_modes );

  radar_longitude += 100000;  //Error - can't modify
  radar_modes.add('Crazy Fast'); //Error - cannot add to an immutable list
}
```

**Example 4.12** instantiates a List literal value at compile time by using the const keyword in conjunction with the literal syntax. This is required for declaring any non-primitive object as a constant. The const List reference is then assigned to a const identifier of radar_modes.

Unlike `final` variables, properties of objects that are marked as a `const` are immutable. You get an error when trying to use the `add()` method on the `List` constant because its values cannot be changed.

## CONSTANT CONSTRUCTORS

Using a `const` constructor allows a class of objects that cannot be defined using a literal syntax to be assigned to a constant identifier.

When using the `const` keyword for initialization, no matter how many times you instantiate an object with the same values, only one instance exists in memory. A constant class shares all the same instantiation restrictions as a constant object.

Class fields that are assigned using a `const` constructor must be marked as `final`. This allows new instances of the class to be instantiated by the `const` keyword or the `new` keyword.

**EXAMPLE 4.13**

```
class Location {
  final int x;
  final int y;
  const Location(this.x, this.y);
}

main() {
  const Location gate = const Location(400, 200);
  const Location tower = const Location(500, 200);
  const Location tube = const Location(400, 200);

  //false – different values results on a new object
  print(gate == tower);

  //true – same class & values results in the same reference
  print(gate == tube);

  Location runway = new Location(400, 200);
  Location tarmac = new Location(500, 200);
  Location field = new Location(400, 200);
  print(runway == tarmac); //false – new keyword results on a new object
  print(runway == field); //false – new keyword results on a new object
}
```

In **Example 4.13**, you see that anything instantiated with the new keyword is going to create a new instance in memory, and despite matching values, these objects will be unique. You also see that objects that are created with the const keyword and that have the same values evaluate as equal objects. This is because they share the same constant object in memory.

# CLASS INHERITANCE

Inheritance is a paradigm in programming languages that allows objects to share traits similarly to how a human child inherits a trait from a parent. If a father has green eyes, his son might inherit that trait. If a daughter has blonde hair, one of her parents or grandparents contributed the gene, allowing her to inherit the blonde hair.

In a classical programming language, inheritance allows a family of objects to share behavior and properties between related classes of objects.

So far you've learned about the structure of a single class. Being a classical language, Dart supports single inheritance on a class-by-class basis. Single inheritance means that a class can directly inherit from only one class at a time.

You've already been using *implicit inheritance.* If no extended class is defined, all classes in Dart automatically extend the class Object. Dart implements inheritance when the extends keyword is placed after the class name declaration followed by a named identifier of the class which is to be inherited from.

Over the next few sections, you're going to define the taxonomy of a fleet of flying vehicles. You'll start with the most generic and work your way to the most specific.

Let's create a base class of type Vehicle (**Example 4.14**).

**EXAMPLE 4.14**

```
class Vehicle extends Object {
  void turnOn(){
    print('--Turns On--');
  }

  void turnOff(){
      print('--Turns Off--');
    }
}
```

So far this looks like the classes you've already been working with. You'll notice that you've declared two methods, turnOn() and turnoff(). These actions are a common trait of almost any vehicle, so they go into the base class. You will notice that the constructor method is left off. Dart will implicitly provide a constructor with no parameters. Let's evolve the Vehicle class by using inheritance and by defining a new class (**Example 4.15**).

**EXAMPLE 4.15**

```
class Aircraft extends Vehicle {
  String name = "Aircraft";
  String fuelType;
  String propulsion;
  int maxspeed;

  void goForward() {
    print('--$name moves forward--');
  }
}
```

By using the keyword extends, you're declaring that a class of Aircraft should acquire all the fields and default behavior provided in class Vehicle. You then define properties that would be common traits of all Aircraft. Let's take a look at an implementation in **Example 4.16**.

**EXAMPLE 4.16**

```
 main() {
  Aircraft craft = new Aircraft(); //uses the implicit class constructor
  craft.turnOn(); //inherits from Vehicle
  craft.goForward(); //defined only in Aircraft
  craft.turnOff(); //inherits from Vehicle
}

//Output:
//--Turns On--
//--Aircraft moves forward--
//--Turns Off--
```

Next, let's assume that when speaking, a person wouldn't say, "I'm going to go for a ride in my aircraft." A listener might infer some of the behaviors associated with that statement, but it's still vague. An aircraft can be many things. Instead, they would refer to something more concrete, such as a blimp or a plane. You don't have enough details in the Aircraft class in Example 4.16, so you're going to declare Aircraft as an abstract class and build out a more concrete implementation with a few different types of aircraft.

## ABSTRACT CLASSES

An abstract class in Dart is a class used to share behavior among descendent classes. Abstract classes cannot be directly instantiated. You're going to prefix the existing class declaration using the abstract keyword.

```
abstract class Aircraft extends Vehicle {

  ...

  ...

}
```

In the implementation from Example 4.16, on the line with new Aircraft(), there is now an error: 'Abstract classes cannot be created with a 'new' expression'. To fix this, let's create some concrete implementations of Aircraft:

**EXAMPLE 4.17**

```
class Blimp extends Aircraft
{
  Blimp(int maxspeed) //explicit class constructor
  {
    this.maxspeed = maxspeed; //assigns values to superclass fields
    this.name = "Blimp"; //assigns values to superclass fields
  }
}

main() {
  Aircraft craft = new Blimp(73);
  craft.turnOn();
  craft.goForward();
  craft.turnOff();
}

//Ouput:
//--Turns On--
//--Blimp moves forward--
//--Turns Off—
```

**Example 4.17** creates a concrete class Blimp. Class Blimp inherits from Aircraft, which inherits from the Vehicle class. Blimp has an explicit class constructor that has a parameter of maxspeed. The class Blimp has a namespace that now includes the inherited fields from each of the parent classes.

# POLYMORPHISM

**FIGURE 4.1**
Inheritance chain and
class interfaces

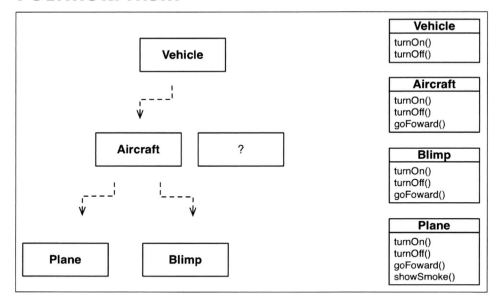

Although Example 4.17 instantiates an instance of class Blimp, you assign the object to a variable of type Aircraft. Dart supports polymorphism. *Polymorphism* allows a family of objects to adhere to a single interface while allowing different implementations. Let's add another concrete class named Plane (**Figure 4.1**).

**EXAMPLE 4.18**

```
class Plane extends Aircraft
{
  Plane()
  {
    this.maxspeed = 537;
    this.name = "Plane";
  }

  void showSmoke()
  {
    print('--Show Smoke--');
  }
}
```

```
main() {
  Aircraft craft;
  craft = new Blimp(73);
  craft.turnOn();
  craft.goForward();
  craft.turnOff();

  craft = new Plane();
  craft.turnOn();
  craft.goForward();
  craft.turnOff();
}

//Output:
//--Turns On--
//--Blimp moves forward--
//--Turns Off--

//--Turns On--
//--Plane moves forward--
//--Turns Off--
```

**Example 4.18** defines a new concrete implementation named Plane, which, just like Blimp, also extends the class Aircraft. The main() function declares a local variable of type Aircraft.

Using polymorphism, you can instantiate Blimp and Plane and assign them to the variable of type Aircraft. Since both are descendants of Aircraft, you can act upon their shared properties. Each object instance retains its own distinctive class properties and instance values, and their output is unique to each object's respective class instance.

Plane implements a custom method of showSmoke(), which is not part of the parent class Aircraft. This means that although you have an instance of Plane, the variable of type Aircraft does not know about Plane's implementation. If you want to access showSmoke() through a variable, you will have to assign the Plane instance to a variable of type Plane.

```
main() {
...
//craft.showSmoke(); //The method 'showSmoke' is not defined for the class
Plane aPlane = new Plane();
aPlane.showSmoke(); //prints --Show Smoke --
}
```

# ABSTRACT METHODS

An *abstract method* establishes an interface but cannot contain execution details. Any subclasses must have their own implementation for a declared abstract method.

To declare a method as abstract, do not use the curly braces in your abstract class (**Example 4.19**). The containing class must also be marked as abstract.

**EXAMPLE 4.19**

```
abstract class Being extends Object
{
  Being()
  {
    print('-- Init Being--');
  }

  //this is an example of an abstract method - no execution statement
  void exist();
}


class Human extends Being
{
  void exist(){
    print('I am I'); //this is the implementation in the subclass
  }
}


main()
{
  Being woman = new Human();

  //woman is a variable with an abstract class type with a concrete instance
  woman.exist();
}
```

When you implement a concrete class that descends from a superclass with an abstract method, if the required method is not yet defined the interpreter will alert you that `'Missing concrete implementation of exist'`. This alerts all subclasses that there is an expectation that they implement the abstract method.

# SUPER CONSTRUCTORS

Part of inheritance is defining the hierarchy of object instantiation. The super() method on a class constructor allows a subclass to pass arguments and execute the constructor of its superclass. The super() method is accessed using a semicolon delimiter off the constructor method, like this:

```
Constructor():super()
```

Super constructors give the subclass the flexibility to custom-tailor constructor parameters and initialize its own class fields. The parameters are passed from the outside in, with the top-most class in the hierarchy being instantiated first.

## IMPLICIT SUPER

If no parameters are defined in a superclass constructor, you can bypass the call to :super() in your subclass. The superclass constructor in **Example 4.20** will be called implicitly.

**EXAMPLE 4.20**

```
abstract class Vertebrate extends Object
{
  Vertebrate()
  {
    print('Vertebrate is: Spined');
  }
}

class Cat extends Vertebrate
{
  Cat () //an implicit call to :super() occurs prior to executing constructor
  {
    print("Cat Is: Alive");
  }
}

main()
{
  Cat pet = new Cat ();
}
```

```
//Output:
//Vertebrate is: Spined
//Cat Is: Alive
```

Upon Cat instantiation, the superclass constructor for Vertebrate is implicitly executed. Upon the completion of the Vertebrate constructor, control is passed back to the descendant class Cat constructor.

## EXPLICIT SUPER()

If your constructors define parameters, you must make a call to :super() via the subclass constructor and provide the requested arguments (**Figure 4.2**).

**EXAMPLE 4.21**

```
abstract class Vertebrate extends Object
{
 Vertebrate(String action)
  {
    print('Vertebrate is: $action'); //first statement executed
  }
}


abstract class Bird extends Vertebrate
{
  Bird(String action):super('Spined')
  {
    print('Bird is: $action');
  }
}


class Finch extends Bird
{
  String color;
  Finch(this.color):super('Winged')
  {
    print('Finch is: $color');
  }
}
```

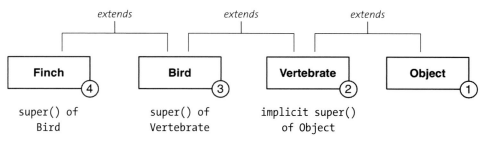

**FIGURE 4.2**
Inheritance chain and execution order

```
main()
{
    Bird animal = new Finch("Yellow");
}

//Output:
//Vertebrate is: Spined
//Bird is: Winged
//Finch is: Yellow
```

In **Example 4.21**, you see the instantiation of a Finch object with an argument of Yellow. The argument Yellow will eventually be assigned to the field color inside of class Finch.

Assignment of field color will occur after the classes higher in the inheritance chain have finished instantiation. The statement :super('Winged') is interpreted prior to the instantiation of class Finch. The statement :super('Spined') is interpreted prior to the instantiation of class Bird.

Once you reach the top-most class in the hierarchy, the Vertebrate constructor statement is executed. Upon the completion of the Vertebrate constructor, control is passed back to the descendant class constructors in a "last in, first out" order.

> **NOTE:** Instantiation of **Object** occurs first. **Object** uses an implicit unparameterized constructor, so no call to **Object():super()** is needed.

# INTERFACES

An interface enforces that a class implements a set list of public fields and methods.

Each class, by default, defines its own interface composed of public fields and methods. Dart has the ability to implement several interfaces. The keyword `implements` allows a class to adhere to multiple interfaces and increase an object's polymorphic range.

The keyword `implement` is followed by an existing named class whose public fields then become implementation requirements for the current class. Let's reuse the code from Example 4.21 and have the `Finch` class implement the abstract class `Being` as an interface.

**NOTE:** It's important to remember that Dart supports only single inheritance, and inheritance shares behavior between classes. Interfaces do not share behavior.

You decide that you want your feathered friends to have the same rights as their human counterparts. You're going to use the `Being` class from Example 4.19 as an interface for class `Finch`. The `Being` class has an object surface area with one abstract method, named `exist()`. The `Finch` class is already inheriting from class `Bird`.

To make `Finch` a `Being`, you're going to implement the `Being` interface in **Example 4.22**.

**EXAMPLE 4.22**

```
abstract class Being
{
  Being()
  {
    print('-- Init Being--');
  }

  void exist();
}

abstract class Vertebrate extends Object
{
 Vertebrate(String action)
  {
    print('Vertebrate is: $action');
  }
}
```

```
abstract class Bird extends Vertebrate
{
  Bird(String action):super('Spined')
  {
    print('Bird is: $action');
  }
}

class Finch extends Bird implements Being
{
  String color;
  Finch(this.color):super('Winged')
  {
    print('Finch is : ' + this.color.toString() );
  }

  void exist()
  {
    print('--I am a $color Finch--');
  }
}

main() {
  Being aBeing = new Finch("yellow");
  aBeing.exist();  //prints --I am a Yellow Finch--

  Bird aBird = new Finch("Yellow");
  aBeing = aBird as Being;
  aBeing.exist(); //prints --I am a Yellow Finch--

  print( aBird is Bird ); //prints true
  print( aBird is Finch ); //prints true
  print( aBird is Vertebrate ); //prints true
  print( aBird is Being ); //prints true
}
```

An interface does not share behavior and defines only available fields and methods. If you do not implement the fields required from the interface, you will receive an error.

Let's see what happens if the class Being changes to a concrete implementation (**Example 4.23**), while leaving it as the interface for class Finch.

**EXAMPLE 4.23**

```
class Being extends Object
{
  Being()
  {
    print('-- Init Being--');
  }

  void exist() {
    print('--I am Being and I exist--');
  }
}

main() {
  Being aBeing = new Finch("yellow");
  aBeing.exist(); //still prints --I am a Yellow Finch--
}
```

Even if you change class Being to a concrete class, with a concrete implementation of exists(), the change will have no effect on the classes that implement its interface. Again, interfaces do not share behavior; they only enforce available fields.

## MIXINS

Dart supports mixins using the with keyword. Mixins allow you to share behavior between unrelated classes. A class that is "mixed in" must be constructed with the following rules:

- The class that is being mixed into another class must be a direct descendent of Object. It must not extend another class.
- It does not define any constructor parameters and never makes an explicit call to super().

By avoiding inheritance and class constructor requirements, mixins become candidates to append additional behavior to any class of object.

Let's create a Bacteria class that uses a generic mixin named `Printify`. The `Printify` mixin (**Example 4.24**) will append the print convention that you've been using to allow objects to talk in their own voice. These `print` statements included a prefix and suffix String.

**EXAMPLE 4.24**

```
class Printify
{
  String sides = '--';
  void say(String output) {
    print('$sides $output $sides');
  }
}


class Bacteria extends Object with Printify
{
  Bacteria()
  {
    say(".....");
  }
}


main() {
  Bacteria life = new Bacteria();  //prints -- ..... --
}
```

In the terrifying circumstance where `Bacteria` becomes self aware, you decide to make `Bacteria` a descendant of the concrete class of `Being` (**Example 4.25**). You can do this because the `Printify` functionality is *mixed in* and is in no way a member of the inheritance chain.

**EXAMPLE 4.25**

```
class Bacteria extends Being with Printify
{
  Bacteria()
  {
    say("I am Bacteria");
  }
}
```

```dart
main() {
  Bacteria life = new Bacteria();
  life.exist();
}

//Output:
//-- Init Being--
//-- I am Bacteria --
//-- I am Being and I exist--
```

## SUMMARY

In this chapter, you've gone from working with single variable instances to working with complex object hierarchies. You've looked at various approaches to sharing behaviors, encapsulating data, and controlling value states.

The next chapter looks at how to share the classes using packages and libraries.

### YOU SHOULD NOW KNOW:

- The difference between a local variable and a class field
- About function scope and class scope
- How class namespace works, and how it interacts with lexical scope
- How to define a class using generative constructors and parameter initialization
- How to define a class using factory constructors
- What the factory keyword implies about object instantiation
- How to define static functionality
- The impact of variable assignments using the keywords `final` and `const`
- How to define class taxonomies using classical inheritance
- The implications of using the `abstract` keyword on classes and methods
- What polymorphism is and how to leverage it
- How to share behavior using inheritance, mixins, and interfaces

# CHAPTER 5

# Packages and Libraries

Libraries are powerful tools for creating and distributing components in Dart. Libraries give you an additional level of abstraction to reuse your classes and methods, while keeping your namespace clean and your designs modular. Libraries are also the foundation for Dart's package system, Pub. It is Dart's central repository for shared packages. This chapter looks at the constructs around libraries, their directory structures, and how to convert them to packages and publish them. Libraries help you adhere to the "separation of concern" principle, which advises breaking your code into distinct units, where each unit is an expert on only one subject.

Since the first launch of your application, you've been using libraries in Dart. When you define your application entry point file, you are loading an implicit library into the Dart VM.

# YOUR FIRST LIBRARY

**FIGURE 5.1**
Directory view

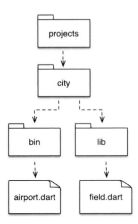

In this chapter, you will build out two libraries and explore the access modifiers that Dart gives you to properly encapsulate your code. One library will be the primary application, named `airport`, and it will request functionality from a library named `field`.

To start, you'll set up this chapter's project to mirror the structure in **Figure 5.1**.

1. Navigate to your `~/projects` folder on your operating system.

2. Create a folder named `city`.

3. Open the JetBrains IDEA Editor.

4. Select Open from the splash screen, or select Open from under the File menu.

5. In the dialog, navigate to your `~/projects` folder.

6. Highlight the `city` folder, and click Choose to select it.

   This imports your `city` project folder into IDEA. Next, you'll create some folders inside your `city` project folder.

7. On the left side of the editor in the IDE's Project panel, Control-click the `city` folder, and choose New > Directory. Name the new directory `bin`.

8. Create another new directory inside your `airline` folder, and name it `lib`.

9. Navigate into the `city` folder on the left side of the editor. Then, inside your `bin` folder, create a file named `airport.dart`.

10. Navigate into the `city` folder on the left side of the editor. Then, inside your `lib` folder, create a file, and name it `field.dart`.

    The resulting directory structure should look like Figure 5.1.

11. Add the code from **Example 5.1** to the `airport.dart` file.

    The example includes the declaration of a `library`, with a named identifier of `airport`. The code is a basic application entry point like you have used throughout the book.

**EXAMPLE 5.1**

```
library airport;

main() {
  print( 'Welcome To The City Airport' );
}
```

12. Run airport.dart.

   There is no discernible effect at run time, but you've just declared a library named airport. Let's create a second library and make it accessible to your airport library.

13. Open the field.dart file from the lib folder inside your city projects folder.

14. Add the code in **Example 5.2**.

**EXAMPLE 5.2**

```
library field;

void gotoField(){
  print('--goto air field--');
}
class Hangar{
  Hangar(){
    print('--init hangar--');
  }
  void openDoor(){
    print('--open hangar door--');
  }
}
class Toolbox{
  Toolbox(){
    print('--init Toolbox--');
  }
  void openLid(){
    print('--open Toolbox Lid--');
  }
}
```

## LIBRARY

Example 5.2 uses the keyword library with a named identifier of field to define a new library. Within the field library's scope, you have two classes and a method. You can now share this with your airport library as seen in **Example 5.3**.

**EXAMPLE 5.3**

```
library airport;
import '../lib/field.dart';
main() {
  print( 'Welcome To The City Airport' );
  gotoField(); //Function member of library field – exposed on import field.dart
  Hangar aHangar = new Hangar(); //Class Hangar is member of library field
  Toolbox portbox = new Toolbox(); //Class Toolbox is member of library field
}


//Output:
//Welcome To The City Airport
//--goto air field--
//--init hangar--
//--init Toolbox--
```

## IMPORT

Example 5.3 introduces the concept of an import keyword. An import uses a relative path to load the targeted file's members into the current library's scope. You now have class Hangar, class Toolbox, and function gotoField() exposed to the current namespace (**Figure 5.2**). To follow the metaphor, an airport is a busy place with many elements; it includes a field, but a field is such a complex area of an airport that it warrants its own domain expert.

Dart allows you to assign an imported library to its own named identifier. This allows you to avoid namespace collisions, or to simply keep track of what library a caller is accessing (**Example 5.4**).

**EXAMPLE 5.4**

```
library airport;
import '../lib/field.dart' as theField;

main() {
  print( 'Welcome To The City Airport' );
  //Function member of library field – exposed on import field.dart
  theField.gotoField();

  //Class Hangar is member of library field
  theField.Hangar aHangar = new theField.Hangar();

  //Class Toolbox is member of library field
  theField.Toolbox portbox = new theField.Toolbox();
}
```

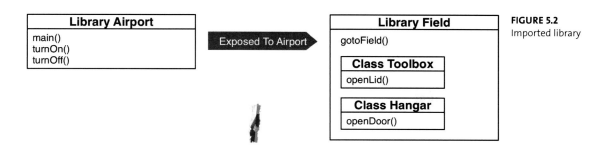

**FIGURE 5.2**
Imported library

## HIDE AND SHOW

The keywords hide and show act as modifiers to the import statement. They allow you to pick and choose a subset of functionality from an imported file, and expose only the named items to the current namespace. Using this approach, the calling library can control the exposure of methods, classes, and variables from the targeted file.

Modify your main() function to match the code in **Example 5.5**:

**EXAMPLE 5.5**

```dart
library airport;
import '../lib/field.dart' show gotoField show Hangar;

main() {
  print( 'Welcome To The City Airport' );
  gotoField();

  Hangar aHangar = new Hangar();
  Toolbox portbox = new Toolbox(); //Error: Undefied class 'Toolbox'
}
```

In Example 5.5, you are using the show keyword to expose only function gotoField and class Hangar. The other members from field.dart are ignored, including class Toolbox. This results in an error when instantiating class Toolbox. You can achieve similar results using the keyword hide in **Example 5.6**.

**EXAMPLE 5.6**

```dart
library airport;
import '../lib/field.dart' hide Toolbox;

main() {
  print( 'Welcome To The City Airport' );
  gotoField();
```

```
  Hangar aHangar = new Hangar();
  Toolbox portbox = new Toolbox(); //Error: Undefined class 'Toolbox'
}
```

In Example 5.6, you are using the hide keyword to explicitly remove class Toolbox. The other members from field.dart are still exposed.

## VISIBILITY AND PRIVACY

Dart has privacy on a library level to help assist with object encapsulation. This means you can designate library members as private, and they will not be exposed to the external libraries that implement them.

To mark a member as private, simply prefix the named identifier with an underscore. This stands in contrast to many other C-style languages, which enable privacy on a class level and use specific keywords, such as private or public, to designate the exposure of their members.

1.  Using **Example 5.7**, add some fence functionality to the field.dart library.

    **EXAMPLE 5.7** field.dart
    ```
    library field;

    String _fenceKey= "A1B2C3";

    void openFence(key) {
      if(key == _fenceKey) {
        print('--fence swings open--');
      }
    }

    void gotoField() {
      print('--goto hangar--');
      openFence(_fenceKey);
    }

    class Hangar{
      Hangar(){
        print('--init hangar--');
      }
    ```

```
  void openDoor(){
    print('--open hangar door--');
  }
}

class Toolbox{
  Toolbox(){
    print('--init Toolbox--');
  }

  void openLid(){
    print('--open Toolbox Lid--');
  }
}
```

Example 5.7 declared a string variable named _fenceKey. By prefixing the name with an underscore, you are initializing it as a private member of the field library. Because scope is on a library level, all members in the field library have _fenceKey accessible in their namespace.

2.  Modify the airport.dart to run the new fence functionality (**Example 5.8**).

**EXAMPLE 5.8** airport.dart

```
library airport;
import '../lib/field.dart';

main() {
  print( 'Welcome To The City Airport' );
  gotoField();

  Hangar aHangar = new Hangar();
  Toolbox portbox = new Toolbox();
}

//Output:
//Welcome To The City Airport
//--goto hangar--
//--fence swings open--
//--init hangar--
//--init Toolbox--
```

**FIGURE 5.3**
Imported library with
private fields

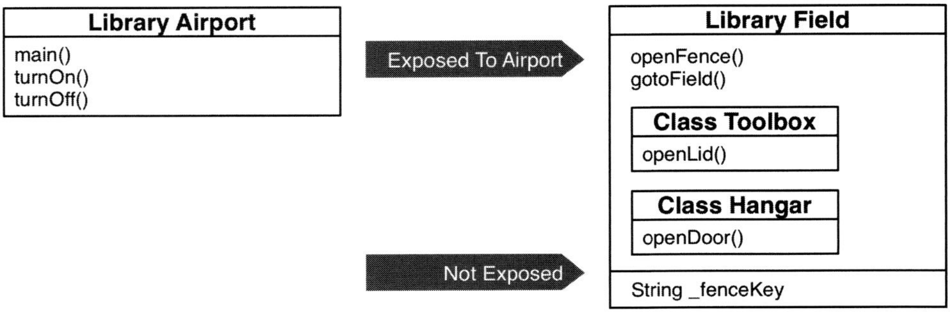

| Library Airport |
|---|
| main() |
| turnOn() |
| turnOff() |

Exposed To Airport

| Library Field |
|---|
| openFence() |
| gotoField() |

| **Class Toolbox** |
|---|
| openLid() |

| **Class Hangar** |
|---|
| openDoor() |

Not Exposed

String _fenceKey

3. Run the app. The fence successfully swings open.

4. Try to access that same key, but from the airport library as shown in **Example 5.9**.

**EXAMPLE 5.9**

```
library airport;
import '../lib/field.dart';

main() {
  print( 'Welcome To The City Airport' );
  gotoField();

  Hangar aHangar = new Hangar();
  Toolbox portbox = new Toolbox();
  openFence(_fenceKey); //undefined name _fenceKey
}
```

In Example 5.9, you see that the function openFence() from the library field is exposed to the airport library. However, when you try to access the variable _fenceKey from field, you get an undefined error. This is expected. As illustrated by **Figure 5.3**, the member openFence is public, and the member _fenceKey is private and thus not available to the external library airport.

5. Delete the broken line containing openFence() to fix this problem.

   Privacy rules are all-inclusive; you are either a member of the library and have access to private members, or you are not part of the library and do not know the members exist.

6. Modify the functionality of class Toolbox and function gotoField, from Example 5.9, to match **Example 5.10**.

**EXAMPLE 5.10**

```
library field;
...

class Toolbox{

  Toolbox() {
    print('--init Toolbox--');
    openLid();
    _closeLid(); //constructor can access private method from same library
  }

  void _closeLid()
  {
    print('--close Toolbox Lid --');
  }

  void openLid()
  {
    print('--open Toolbox Lid--');
  }
}

void gotoField()
{
  print('--goto air field--');
  Toolbox hangarbox = new Toolbox();
  hangarbox.openLid();
  hangarbox._closeLid();
}
```

Example 5.10 added a private method of _closeLid() to the class Toolbox. The private method can be called by the Toolbox() constructor since the constructor is part of the same library.

A Toolbox instance is instantiated to a local variable inside of function gotoField(). The variable instance hangarbox is also able to execute its _closeLid() method since the instance hangarbox is scoped inside of library field.

7. Modify the airport library to match **Example 5.11**.

This code tries to instantiate an instance of the same Toolbox class to an instance inside library airport. The variables method _closeLid() will not be accessible.

**EXAMPLE 5.11**
```
library airport;
import '../lib/field.dart';

main() {
  print( 'Welcome To The City Airport' );
  gotoField();

  Hangar aHangar = new Hangar();
  Toolbox portbox = new Toolbox();
  portbox.openLid();
  portbox._closeLid(); //Error: _closeLid() is not defined on class Toolbox
}
```

As you can see in Example 5.11, when you use an import statement to load a file into the caller's namespace, you do not get access to the private members from the imported library. Libraries are designed to allow the author to limit the surface area of their exposed interface. This makes distributed libraries clear for other developers to understand.

8. Delete the line that's causing the error.

## PART AND PART OF

The part keyword is similar to import in that part loads the named file into its caller's namespace. However, part expects the loaded file to have a declaration of part of with a value that matches the named library identifier of the caller. This creates a bidirectional pairing between both part and part of.

Dart's part and part of keywords are closely linked to library-level privacy. In Dart, part and part of establish a relationship between a named library and partial library files. When loaded, the part of keyword exposes the loaded files' public and private members to the named library. This allows shared private fields from a library to span across multiple files, while hiding private members from external libraries.

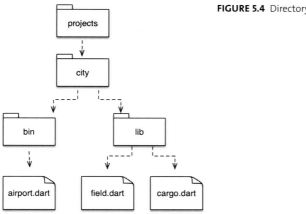

**FIGURE 5.4** Directory view

1. Inside the lib folder, create a partial file named cargo.dart (**Figure 5.4**).

**EXAMPLE 5.12** cargo.dart

```dart
part of field;

void gotoBaggageWindow()
{
  print('--goto the baggage building window--');
}
void _grabBags()
{
  print('--A bag from cargo is passed back--');
}
class Baggage{
    Baggage() {
      print('--Im the bag man - i have a passcode of: $_passcode');
    }
    void tryGrabBag(key)
    {
      if(key == _passcode)
      {
        _grabBags();
      } else {
        print('--Bag man says: you are not authorized');
      }
    }
}
```

In **Example 5.12**, notice that you are declaring the second part of the bidirectional pairing with the part of keyword for a library named field. That means that this partial expects to be loaded into the library field, and that field will have access to all the fields from cargo.dart.

Also notice that you created a private function named _grabBags() and a class of Baggage. Class Baggage is using string interpolation on a variable named _passcode that is not declared in this partial.

2. Load this partial (**Example 5.13**) into the field library in field.dart by appending the following:

**EXAMPLE 5.13** `field.dart`

```
library field;
part "cargo.dart";

String _fenceKey = "A1B2C3";
String _passcode = "007";

void gotoField()
{
  print('--goto air field--');
  _grabBags(); //example of access to cargo.darts private members
}
...
```

In Example 5.13, notice that you loaded the partial library file cargo.dart into library field by using keyword part and not keyword import.

By using part, you not only load the file, but also complete the bidirectional pairing. With the pairing complete, field.dart and cargo.dart are joined together to create a single library named field.

By loading the members from cargo.dart into library field, you've exposed the private method _grabBags() to the rest of library field.

Let's continue the metaphor. Back in library airport, thanks to library access modifiers, patrons who are wandering around do not have access such that they can just grab bags off the field—that would be insecure. Instead, you need to instantiate someone who has access privileges.

3. Update `airport.dart` to match **Example 5.14**.

**EXAMPLE 5.14** `airport.dart`

```
library airport;
import '../lib/field.dart';

main() {
  print( 'Welcome To The City Airport' );
  gotoField(); //member of field.dart - exposed by import library field
  gotoBaggageWindow(); //member of cargo.dart - exposed by import library field
  // _grabBags(); //a private member of library field, not available to airport
  //member of cargo.dart - exposed via library  field
  var bagman = new Baggage();
  //Baggage accesses _passcode defined in  field.dart
  bagman.tryGrabBag('dunno');
  //Baggage accesses _grabBags() defined in  cargo.dart
  bagman.tryGrabBag('007');
}


//Welcome To The City Airport
//--goto air field--
//--A bag from cargo is passed back--
//--goto the baggage building window--
//--Im the bag man - i have a passcode of: 007
//--Bag man says: you are not authorized
//--A bag from cargo is passed back--
```

In Example 5.14, you're back to using the `import` keyword to load `library field` into the namespace of `library airport`. Because this is a `library` importing another `library`, you do not execute a bidirectional handshake that would be required to access the private members of `library field`. However, when you instantiate an instance of a class member of `library field`, such as class Baggage, that instance has access rights to all of `library field`'s private members. When a bagman grabs a bag, he needs to supply the proper key. His first attempt fails because he doesn't know the key. The second attempt passes because the provided string argument matches the value of the private password inside the `field` library.

**NOTE:** Access modifiers prevent access only to objects for your code. It's not a form of computer security to ward off hackers.

# PACKAGES AND PUBSPEC.YAML

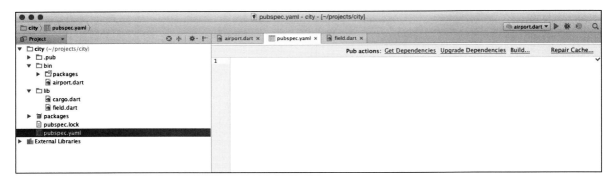

**FIGURE 5.5** pubspec.yaml open in IDEA

Packages in Dart are libraries that you share locally or publicly via the Pub repositories. Pub is a shared repository of third-party packages that can be downloaded and installed at https://pub.dartlang.org. To enable Pub support, a project needs to contain a pubspec.yaml file in the root directory of the project.

pubspec.yaml is a file used by the Pub task runner to both create an inventory of packages and to assign meta information about the project. Once populated, Pub will parse the pubspec.yaml file and fetch the requested remote packages.

YAML expects each object to use a two-space delimiter to separate each of its parent's properties. To append a property to an object, include a colon at the end of the parent object's name, create a new line, and increase the indentation by two spaces.

Let's create the pubspec.yaml on the folder airline:

1. Right-click the city folder.

2. Choose New File.

3. Name the file pubspec.yaml, and open it in IDEA (**Figure 5.5**).

4. In the open file, add the top-level meta information for the package. These are string values with no child attributes.

   - name: city_airport

   - version: 0.0.1

   - description: An airport, with a field, a hangar, and cargo handling

   - author: Jack Murphy jack@rightisleft.com

   - homepage: https://github.com/rightisleft/web_apps_dart

5. Define an environment object.

```
environment:
  sdk: '>=1.0.0 <2.0.0'
```

This will allow you to define the constraints for acceptable versions of the Dart SDK.

6. Define a dependencies object.

```
dependencies:
  browser: '0.10.0'
```

This will allow you to provide a list of versioned external packages to include when building the app for development, and also for when building for distribution. Here you add the browser library containing dart2js.

7. Define a dev_dependencies object.

```
dev_dependencies:
  test: '0.12.3'
```

This is similar to the dependencies, but includes packages only needed for development. We'll include Dart's Unit Testing package so you can test locally, but we'll keep the footprint small in production by excluding it.

The completed pubspec.yaml file should look like **Example 5.15**.

**EXAMPLE 5.15**

```
name: city_airport
version: 0.0.1
description: An airport, with a field, a hangar, and cargo handling
author: Jack Murphy jack@rightisleft.com
homepage: https://github.com/rightisleft/web_apps_dart
environment:
  sdk: '>=1.0.0 <2.0.0'
dependencies:
  browser: '0.10.0'
dev_dependencies:
  test: '0.12.3'
```

As seen in Figure 5.5, in the upper-right corner of IDEA is a series of links describing a few available Pub actions. These are links to the command-line Pub tool.

8. Click Get Dependencies to start Pub, which will download the newly defined package declarations.

You now have a folder named packages in your root directory. It contains the libraries browser and test and all their dependencies. Pub recursively manages each package dependency, meaning that Pub imports not only the browser but all the browser's dependencies and its dependencies' dependencies.

# NAMED PACKAGE IMPORTS

**FIGURE 5.6** Available packages

One of the byproducts of declaring pubspec.yaml is enabling a new approach to importing files. By providing meta information about your package, you told Pub about a new package: city_airport. Pub creates a symlink in the packages folder to expose the files in your lib folder (**Figure 5.6**). This makes city_airport available locally in the same way you'd access a package like test.

In previous sections, you used relative paths to import other libraries. Let's go back to the airport.dart class and modify the previous imports.

The previous import approach was:

```
import '../lib/field.dart';
```

Modify airport.dart to match **Example 5.16**:

**EXAMPLE 5.16**

```
library airport;

import 'package:city_airport/field.dart';

main() {
  print( 'Welcome To The City Airport' );
  gotoField(); //Function member of library field - exposed on import
  ⇢ field.dart

  //Class Hangar is member of library field
  Hangar aHangar = new Hangar();
```

```
//Class Toolbox is member of library field
Toolbox portbox = new Toolbox();
```

}

In **Example 5.16**, the path prefix of package:city_airport/ is a reference to your project's /lib folder. By adhering to the Dart project folder conventions, instead of a relative path, the Dart interpreter allows the lib folder to be referenced by a name value assigned in pubspec.yaml. In this case, it's city_airport.

Using package names allows for easy iterative development and upgrade management if you decide to publish your library. By providing a standard folder convention for your local projects, you can construct meaningful folder hierarchies without having to worry about them conflicting with other packages.

Along with lib, you have been using a folder named bin. Dart's folder convention enforces that files in bin are generally implementations of libraries or other binaries needed to run the application. Files in bin are included in the list of files served by the Pub HTTP Server for use by the current application. However, files in bin are not exposed via the package mechanism either locally or when distributed via the Pub repositories.

In Example 5.16, you see that a package import request is also made for test, which refers to the downloaded package library that is now in your packages folder. The unit testing library test is now exposed as Test to library airport.

## SUMMARY

This chapter looked at the power of libraries and packages. Packages are one of the more important concepts to grasp, because they allow you to leverage the third-party software that makes the Dart platform so powerful.

### YOU SHOULD NOW KNOW:

- How to define a library
- How to import a library
- How to assign a library to a custom named identifier
- How to expose specific fields from a library using show and hide
- How to use access modifiers in a library
- How to break apart a library into multiple parts
- How to use pubspecy.yaml and pub to acquire packages

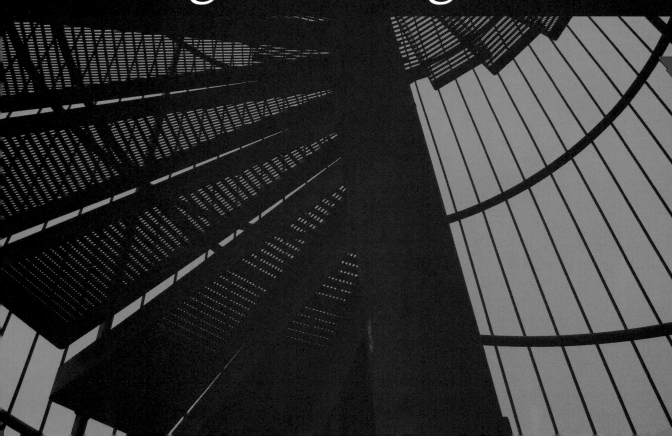

# CHAPTER 6

# Event Loops and Asynchronous Programming

Asynchronous programming is at the core of modern web application development for both front-end and back-end developers. Dart has a great set of tools that allow you to interact with remote services and to write non-blocking code. This chapter looks at the Dart event loop and how to write asynchronous requests.

# CONCURRENT COMPUTING PARADIGM

Dart is single threaded. This means that, by default, only a single CPU process is associated with the Dart VM. Having only one process means that your Dart code will execute in a linear fashion and won't be disrupted. This produces a challenge for developers who are trying to load data from other sources.

Let's imagine that you have a timer that is displaying a countdown until New Year's Eve. At exactly midnight, a video of fireworks will play. The associated video file is roughly 100 MB and becomes available only 30 seconds before midnight. You want to load the video into memory so it's available to play right as the countdown hits midnight.

If your code were always forced to load in a linear fashion, an action such as loading a 100 MB video file from the file system would result in the Dart VM pausing all other execution while the file was being read from the file system and loaded into memory. This is referred to as a *synchronous request*, and would result in your countdown pausing while the video file was loading. By modern development standards, this is an unacceptable user experience.

To manage these types of tasks, the Dart run time executes on what's known as a *concurrent computing paradigm*. Concurrent computing breaks apart a single process into several queues, with each queue having its own responsibility. Together, these queues are referred to as the *event loop*.

Lots of time is spent writing code that is appended to Dart's *event queue*, which is one of many types of queues in Dart's concurrency model. The Dart VM has other responsibilities outside the event queue that are hidden from developers, such as memory management, garbage collection, operating system interactions, and other low-level VM tasks.

If you structure your code using non-blocking functions, the Dart VM happily lets the rest of your application continue executing inside the event queue while the VM is off doing the heavy lifting of interacting with the operating system. These non-blocking functions are known as *asynchronous requests*. Asynchronous requests inside the event loop are usually implemented using futures, completers, and streams.

# FUTURES, COMPLETERS, AND STREAMS

To understand the execution order of a synchronous request versus an asynchronous request, let's start with a synchronous file system call.

## SYNCHRONOUS REQUESTS

Dart's naming conventions for synchronous requests have a named suffix of *Sync() for method names. The suffix indicates that the method will block all other code execution until the result of the request is in memory (**Example 6.1**).

**EXAMPLE 6.1**

```dart
import 'dart:io';
main() {
  File pub = new File('pubspec.yaml');
  print ( pub.readAsStringSync() );
  print('-- Logger --');
}


//Output:
//name: city_airport
//version: 0.0.1
//description: An airport, with a field, a hangar, and cargo handling
//author: Jack Murphy jack@rightisleft.com
//homepage: https://github.com/rightisleft/web_apps_dart
//environment:
//  sdk: '>=1.0.0 <2.0.0'
//dependencies:
//  browser: '0.10.0'
//dev_dependencies:
//  test: '0.12.3'
//-- Logger --
```

A benefit of using a blocking request is that the requested data is treated as if it were already stored in memory. No additional asynchronous load handling control structures are needed, because the execution context does not move ahead until the function readAsStringSync() is completed.

In the output, you should see the contents of pubspec.yaml written out before the print() statement.

## FUTURES

A *future* is a paradigm in asynchronous development that allows an object to delay the execution of a callback function until a specified task has completed. By deferring execution, the run time is allowed to continue running the rest of the application code until the future's completion criteria are met. Upon completion, the previously defined callback function executes. This is ideal for making asynchronous requests for external data. Let's take a look at the future method `File.readAsString()`.

**EXAMPLE 6.2**

```dart
import 'dart:io';
main() {
  File aFile = new File('pubspec.yaml');
  aFile.readAsString().then(aCallback);
  print('--Logger--');
}


void aCallback(String text){
  print(text);
}


//Output
//-- Logger --
//name: jit_airlines
//version: 0.0.1
//author: Jack Murphy
//description: Building Modern Web Application with Dart
//environment:
//  sdk: '>=1.0.0 <2.0.0'
//dependencies:
//  http_server: any
```

A future exposes a method named `then()`, which accepts a function reference as an argument. While the Dart VM is loading the text file into memory, the execution of the rest of the application continues. Once the whole external file finishes loading, the reference executes with the loaded data now available as a supplied argument.

In **Example 6.2**, in the Output you can see that even though `readAsString()` executes prior to the `Logger` statement, `Logger` is printed before the contents of `pubspec.yaml`. This occurs because execution of the function `aCallback()` is deferred until task completion; in this case, task completion occurs after `pubspec.yaml` is finished loading into memory.

# FUTURES AND COMPLETERS

You can implement your own asynchronous functions by using instances of class Future and class Completer. You saw in Example 6.2 that a future creates a contract to ensure a callback function executes after a task is completed. Let's wrap an expensive processing task inside a future and defer its execution.

**EXAMPLE 6.3**

```dart
import 'dart:async';
main() {
  expensiveCalc().then(aCallback);
  print('-- Logger --');
}

void aCallback(int index)
{
  print(index);
}

Future expensiveCalc() {
  Completer c = new Completer();
  num index = 0;
  void expensive() {
    while(index < 1234567890)
    {
      index++;
    }
    c.complete(index);
  }

  expensive();
  return c.future;
}

//Output:
//--Logger--
//1234567890
```

**Example 6.3** introduces the class `Completer`, which is an explicit way to control the flow inside a future. The `Completer` instance has two attributes of interest for this example: `.complete()` and `.future`.

- `Completer.future`: The `future` property allows you to adhere to your contract with the function declaration by returning a new instance of object type `Future`.

- `Completer.complete()`: The contract with `Future` is finished when the `complete()` function is called when the task is done. If the callback function defines a method parameter, the argument must be supplied to the `complete()` method. In Example 6.3, the `aCallback()` function expects an integer, so it is passed through the `complete()` method as an argument.

Just as in the Example 6.2, the future is declared and execution of the callback is deferred. The logger statement executes while the `expensive()` function executes, which is when its turn arrives in the event queue.

## STREAMS

A stream is an asynchronous implementation of an iterator of an unknown length. Unlike futures, streams have no defined completion state. Example 6.2 loaded the file `pubspec.yaml`. The action of loading data has a finite life cycle; the Dart `File` class's method `readAsString()` knows when the end of the file occurs and invokes `complete()`. In contrast, a stream continues to operate until you explicitly remove the listener.

Streams can be useful for listening for multiple events in a non-blocking fashion. Some scenarios in which non-blocking events are used include waiting for a mouse click, an event from a socket connection, or reading the list of contents from a directory. Let's take a look at the directory example.

**EXAMPLE 6.4**

```
import 'dart:io';
main() {
    Directory dir = new Directory('.');
    dir.list().listen(onData);
}

int index = 1;
void onData(FileSystemEntity data) {
  print("$index: -- $data --");
  index++;
}
```

```
//Output:
//1: -- Directory: './.pub' --
//2: -- Directory: './bin' --
//3: -- Directory: './lib' --
//4: -- Directory: './packages' --
//5: -- File: './pubspec.lock' --
//6: -- File: './pubspec.yaml' -
```

In **Example 6.4**, you can see that class `Directory` exposes a method `list()` that is of type Stream. By invoking `Stream`'s method `listen()`, you are able to register a handler that is invoked for each event of a file found in your current working directory. The real power of streams comes into play when you are filtering the contents of the iterable list.

**EXAMPLE 6.5**

```
import 'dart:io';
main() {
  Directory dir = new Directory('.');
  dir.list().where(test).listen(onData);
}


int index = 1;
void onData(FileSystemEntity data) {
  print("$index: -- $data --");
  index++;
}


bool test(FileSystemEntity data){
  return data is Directory;
}


//Output:
//1: -- Directory: './.pub' --
//2: -- Directory: './bin' --
//3: -- Directory: './lib' --
//4: -- Directory: './packages' -
```

**Example 6.5** adds a filter to your stream. The `where()` method is called on every element in the stream, and only the statements that return `true` are passed into the `listen()` handler. Example 6.5 filters out all the objects of type `File`. The `Stream` class has lots of very powerful methods to help you filter your data for processing.

# EVENT LOOP

The Dart event loop is part of the Dart concurrency model. It defines the execution order of tasks throughout your code base. The first event in every application is from your main() root entry point.

The event loop consists of two queue types: the event queue and the microtask queue. Each queue is a "first in, first out" (FIFO) queue. When you instantiate an asynchronous task, Dart adds the deferred execution request to the back of the event queue. That means the newest event in the queue will be executed last.

When the event loop starts, it first executes the events in the microtask queue. The microtask queue is a kind of fast track for the event loop that allows tasks to be executed with priority over normal events in the event queue. This acts as a channel for asynchronous tasks to be completed prior to pulling the next event from the event queue. If a microtask queue didn't exist, any events that were instantiated inside an event would have to wait for the rest of the entire event queue to complete prior to execution.

Let's schedule a microtask:

**EXAMPLE 6.6**
```
import 'dart:async';
main() {
  scheduleMicrotask(() => print('Task A'));
}
```

**Example 6.6** exposes the method scheduleMicrotask() from the dart:async library and passes it a function expression. When several events and microtasks are scheduled, the order of execution becomes clearer.

**EXAMPLE 6.7**
```
import 'dart:async';
main() {
  new Future( () => print('Future 1'));
  print('print I');
  new Future( () => print('Future 2'));
  new Future( () => print('Future 3'));
  scheduleMicrotask(() => print('Task A'));
  new Future( () => print('Future 4'));
  scheduleMicrotask( () => print('Task B'));
  print('print II');
  scheduleMicrotask(() => print('Task C'));
  new Future( () => print('Future 5'));
}
```

```
//Output:
//print I
//print II
//Task A
//Task B
//Task C
//Future 1
//Future 2
//Future 3
//Future 4
//Future 5
```

**Example 6.7** uses a variety of methods that all eventually invoke print(). Although the order in which the methods are declared looks like a rat's nest of code, the output is uniform and follows the order of operations you defined for the event loop:

1. Statements inside the main() function block are executed before any asynchronous tasks.

2. When the call to main() finishes, the event loop starts at the top of both of its queues. It first pulls off and executes tasks from the microtask queue, in the order in which they were added.

3. When the microtask queue is emptied, the event queue begins processing its contents, which is a list of futures, also in the order in which they were added.

## ASYNC

In the "Futures and Completers" section, you saw how to write your own asynchronous functions. Using the Completer class, you explicitly define a Future wrapper and tie it to a Completer object. Although explicit, it's rather verbose. Dart has a reserved async keyword that implicitly implements a future and completer pairing.

The async keyword modifies a function to return a future, and modifies the functionality of the return keyword to behave as if calling Completer.complete.

Let's refactor the expensiveCalc() function from Example 6.3.

### EXAMPLE 6.8
```
import 'dart:async';
main(){
  expensiveCalc().then((index) => print(index) );
  scheduleMicrotask(() => print('MicroTask'));
}
```

```
expensiveCalc() async {
  int index = 0;
  int expensive() {
    while(index < 123456789)
    {
      index++;
    }
    return index;   //returns 123456789
  }


  return expensive(); //returns behaves like Completer.complete
}

//Output:
//MicroTask
//123456789
```

In **Example 6.8**, in your main() function, you're executing two statements:

- expensiveCalc()—The first statement invokes the async method. If you look at the expensiveCalc() implementation, you'll notice that the keyword async is located between the method signature and the function block's opening curly braces.

  A return type is intentionally omitted to illustrate that async converts the declared field into a future. Nowhere in the code do you see a reference to class Future or class Completer.

- scheduleMicrotask()—The second statement creates a microtask event. According to the event loop rules, a microtask always executes prior to a future located on the event queue. This illustrates that the expensiveCalc() function is indeed a future, because the future gets executed *after* the microtask.

As you can see in the output, the microtask executes first, followed by the asynchronous future. You've removed a ton of boilerplate code from the function declaration while maintaining the asynchronous nature of the code.

## AWAIT

Dart has the keyword await, which allows you to take an asynchronous request and simulate blocking synchronously until the future has completed.

This is a bit of syntactic sugar and does not modify the control flow of the Dart run time. To use the await keyword, the function containing the await statement must be designated as async. This results in the containing function being pulled out of the current execution context and placed into the event queue.

Once in the event queue, the containing async block statement executes. This emulates writing synchronous functionality and bypasses the need to work with asynchronous style code (futures).

Let's modify the example to use the await keyword with a traditional Future and Completer implementation.

**EXAMPLE 6.9**

```dart
import 'dart:async';
main(){
  print('1');
  newEvent();
  print('3');
}

newEvent() async {
  print('--new event--');
  print('--2--');
  print ( await expensiveCalcFull() );
}

  Future expensiveCalcFull() {
   Completer c = new Completer();
   num index = 0;
   void expensive() {
     while(index < 1234567890)
     {
       index++;
     }
     c.complete(index);
   }

   expensive();
   return c.future;
  }

//Output:
//1
//3
//--new event--
//--2--
//1234567890
```

As you can see in the output of **Example 6.9**, because of the ordering rules of the event loop, both of the print statements in the main() function execute before any of the asynchronous code inside the newEvent() function executes.

- newEvent()—This function has a modifier keyword of async that turns the function into a future, causing it to be placed onto the event queue for deferred execution.

- await expensiveCalcFull()—This function usually exposes a method that adheres to the class interface for Future, and a callback function is usually required prior to access to the calculated value.

  Because you're modifying the execution using the await keyword, the Dart VM simulates a synchronous operation and waits for the Completer.complete function to be called prior to interpreting the value of the expression. The function's return value reads as being immediately accessible to the caller print().

## SUMMARY

This chapter looked at the different ways to write and handle synchronous and asynchronous code. The following chapters use these techniques frequently. It is important to have a clear understanding of Dart's asynchronous capabilities and of the impact on execution order. These approaches will come in handy when running a web server, requesting RESTful data, or simply wiring up user interfaces and click handlers.

### YOU SHOULD NOW KNOW:

- The impact of synchronous code
- The impact of asynchronous code
- The order of operations in which Dart executes both synchronous and asynchronous code
- The difference between the event queue and the microtask queue
- How to declare a non-blocking function that returns a value when it becomes available
- How to use futures and completers
- How to use, and the impact of, the await and async keywords

# PART II

# Full-Stack App Development with Dart

# CHAPTER 7

# Planning the Application

In this chapter, you will expand Just-In-Time Airlines ticket application to allow consumers to purchase seats on the fictional airline.

# FICTITIOUS COMPANY BACKGROUND

Just-In-Time Airlines is a new regional carrier specializing in discounted one-way flights throughout the state of California. The key to its success is an aircraft design that uses an alternative engine technology.

The engine's power source is said to have nearly zero operating costs for small planes, but because of high temperatures, the planes have an extremely limited range and an extremely long recharge cycle. Even with those limitations, the potential cost savings in the market will allow the company to scale up rapidly once it can prove that its plane design, although terrifying to fly, is safe for consumer use.

Flights operate on a two-directional route between cities, making one round trip per day. This is a small startup, so destinations are limited. The service area includes only five major metro areas inside California: San Diego, Los Angeles, Oakland, San Francisco, and Sacramento. Due to the aircraft's small size, the capacity is seven passenger seats per flight.

The pricing model uses a fixed window for rate hikes. Any booking date more than 15 days out is referred to as a "steal." Booking dates between 14 and 5 days out are referred to as "standard." And anything within 5 days is labeled as "desperate." The rate varies accordingly.

# FEATURE REQUESTS

You have been approached to develop the prototype for the ticketing system and have been delivered the wireframes shown in **Figure 7.1** as a starting point.

You notice that the home page appears to be a static landing page with the following components:

- **Top navigation:** This component shows users their position in the site hierarchy. As with many sites, this top navigation component will persist across all pages on the site.

- **Deep linking:** This functionality allows linking directly to the order page for specific flights from static links.

- **Static content:** Items on the home page are often owned by marketing departments and are not coupled to the core functionality of the app. You've been asked to include some static content: flights represented as graphics with deep links into our full ticketing application.

- **Call to action:** In Figure 7.1, the call to action is the All Flights button, which when clicked takes you to the Flights tab. This is where the core functionality of the ticket purchasing system will exist.

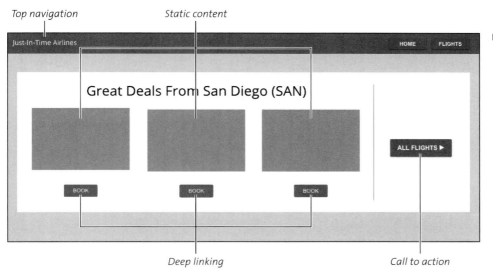

**FIGURE 7.1** Home page

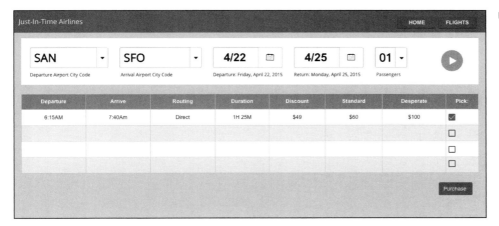

**FIGURE 7.2** Flights

In **Figure 7.2**, you'll notice that there are two primary components that will compose the Flights page:

- **Itinerary picker:** This component allows users to select their departure and arrival information using drop-down menus. The menus are populated with data that coincides with route information for Just-In-Time Airlines. Upon entering all the passenger details, clicking the large circular arrow button should render the available flight information in the flight display.

- **Flight display:** This component retrieves a list of available flights for a specific date and flight route filtered by input parameters.

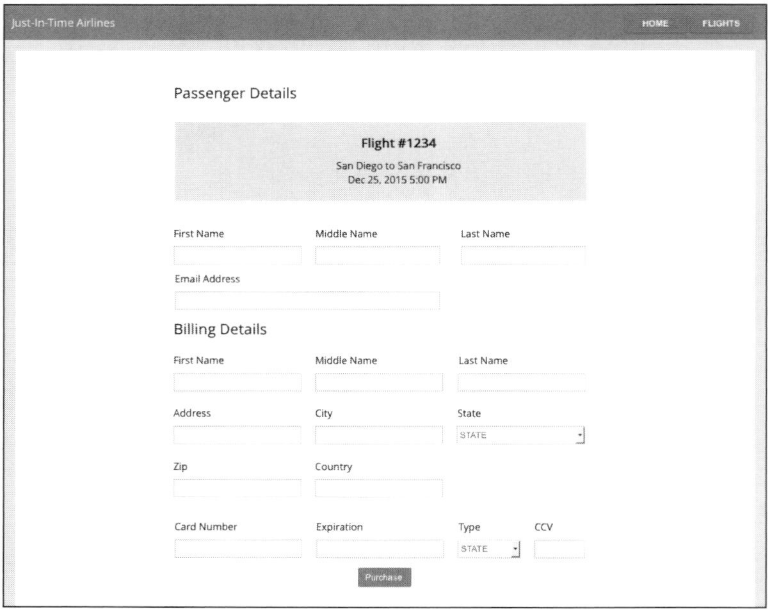

FIGURE 7.3 Order form

Figure 7.3 shows the two primary components that will compose the order form page:

- **Flight box:** This component is based on the URL parameters and displays the selected flight that the user is going to purchase.

- **Order form:** This component allows form handling to complete the purchase transaction of the selected ticket.

The requested features are a loose specification. As the features are built out, you'll be asked to handle some of the interaction design edge cases. They will be called out on a feature-by-feature basis.

## DATA ENTITIES

Before you begin coding, you need the data that will power the Just-In-Time Airlines ticket application. The airline provided you with the initial outline of its database in a spreadsheet. The workbook is separated into multiple sheets to represent each type of data entity. This allows you to take a look at the structure of the data prior to exporting it to a JSON format for your own needs.

**NOTE:** For now, just focus on the application design aspects of the project. We've used a plugin for Google Sheets to export it as JSON. The next chapter will look at the data and source code for this project.

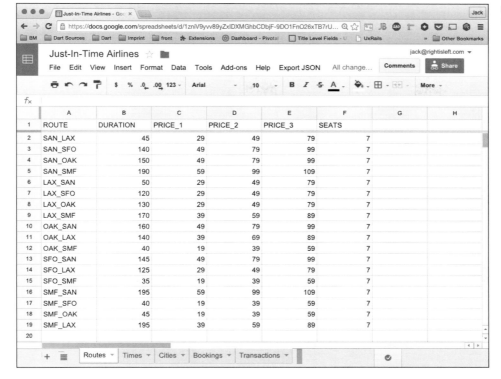

FIGURE 7.4
Routes entity

## ROUTES

A routes entity (**Figure 7.4**) contains service information about the flight:

- ROUTE: Airport code of arrival and airport code of the destination using an underscore delimiter.
- DURATION: The amount of time between takeoff and landing
- PRICE_1: The lowest fair offered, referred to as a "steal"
- PRICE_2: The standard fare offered
- PRICE_3: The last-minute booking price, referred to as "desperate"
- SEATS: The number of tickets that can be sold for the flight regardless of price

FIGURE 7.5
Times entity

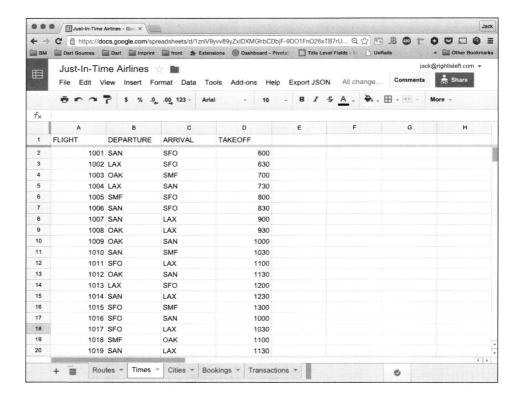

## TIMES

A times entity (**Figure 7.5**) contains data for when a route is executed:

- FLIGHT: The unique identifier for a flight; renews each day
- DEPARTURE: The code for the airport a flight leaves from
- ARRIVAL: The code for the airport a flight lands at
- TAKEOFF: The time at which a flight is scheduled to depart; uses Pacific Standard Time and is displayed in military time (24-hour notation)

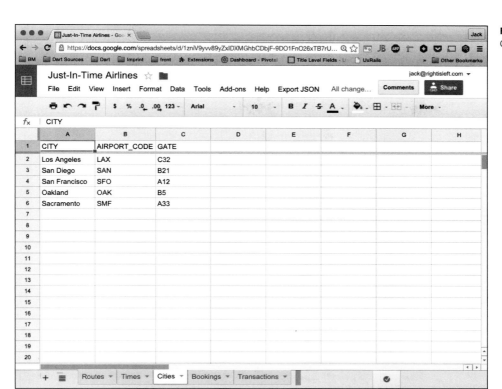

FIGURE 7.6
Cities entity

## CITIES

A cities entity (**Figure 7.6**) contains data for the operating area of all flights:

- CITY: The full name of the city the airport services
- AIRPORT_CODE: Three-letter code for the city's airport
- GATE: Which gate Just-In-Time Airlines flies out of

FIGURE 7.7
Purchases entity

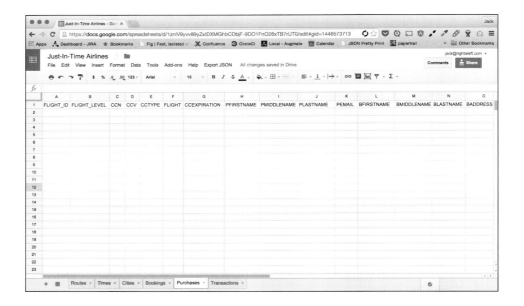

## PURCHASES

A purchases entity (**Figure 7.7**) contains data for the passenger, the booked flight, and associated billing information. It's the data representation of the order form from the layout in Figure 7.3. It's important to note that the purchases entity will be user generated. That means you will not have any seed data related to purchases:

- FLIGHTID: The unique ID of the flight purchased
- FLIGHTLEVEL: The pricing tier for the ticket
- CCN: The credit card number used in the transaction (demo purposes only)
- CCV: The security number on the backside of the user's card
- CCTYPE: The brand of the credit card used, such as Visa, MasterCard, and so on
- CCEXPIRATION: The date on which the credit card expires
- PFIRSTNAME: The passenger's first name
- PMIDDLENAME: The passenger's middle name
- PLASTNAME: The passenger's last name
- PEMAIL: The passenger's email address
- BFIRSTNAME: The first name on the credit card

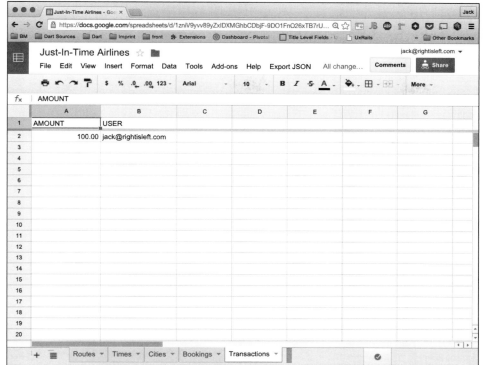

FIGURE 7.8
Transactions entity

- BMIDDLENAME: The middle name on the credit card
- BLASTNAME: The last name on the credit card
- BADDRESS: The mailing address associated with the credit card
- BCITY: The city address associated with the credit card
- BSTATE: The state associated with the credit card
- BZIP: The zip code associated with the credit card
- BCOUNTRY: The country in which the credit card was issued

## TRANSACTIONS

A transactions entity (**Figure 7.8**) contains data for the passenger and for the amount spent:

- USER: The email address to identify the user
- AMOUNT: The total cost the passenger pays for the flight

# ARCHITECTURE CHOICES

Now that you have an understanding of what the application needs to do and what the business constraints are, let's make some decisions about what architecture to use. The following is a list of libraries that will be used in the following chapters:

- **Database:** You'll use the Mongo database to persist the data. Dart has a great community library named mongo_dart, which you'll use to interact with MongoDB on the server side.

  https://pub.dartlang.org/packages/mongo_dart

- **API server:** You'll use Shelf to power your RESTful API. Shelf is a middleware library that allows you to compose multiple components together to create a lean and powerful server application. You'll use the Shelf IO and Shelf Router components as starting points for your server application.

  https://pub.dartlang.org/packages/shelf

  https://pub.dartlang.org/packages/shelf_route

- **Web server:** You'll use Pub to build your Dart assets and deploy them using Shelf and Shelf Static.

  https://pub.dartlang.org/packages/shelf_static

- **Client framework:** You'll use Angular 2 Dart for web components and client-side routing. You'll use the Dart:Html libraries for generating static assets for the marketing department.

  https://pub.dartlang.org/packages/angular2

- **Style sheets:** You'll build your project using Dart Sass as a CSS preprocessor to write clean, concise CSS.

  https://pub.dartlang.org/packages/sass

- **Data transfer objects:** Dart is running on both the client and server, which means you can share native data structures. You'll use Dartson to serialize and deserialize between native Dart objects. JSON will be used as the data structure of choice while in transport over the wire.

  https://pub.dartlang.org/packages/dartson

**NOTE:** The libraries listed have been carefully selected because they are mature community projects. Some of the projects listed are actively developed by Google engineers but are not official Google projects.

**NOTE:** This book's goal is to give you a solid foundation for writing full-stack Dart applications. Many developers prefer to work with some sort of MVC-based framework. MVC (model–view–controller) is an architectural pattern that helps many developers implement their applications in accordance with the "separation of concerns" principle.

Some great server-side Dart community MVC frameworks are available, but they more often than not need complete buy-in from the entire application. This results in quite a bit of domain-specific knowledge. Instead of using the frameworks, you'll be introduced to the individual components that many of those frameworks leverage.

## SUMMARY

This chapter provided an overview of the project you will be building throughout the rest of the book. The project requirements intentionally do not require a robust modern language, but you'll see that even for simple web applications, Dart is an excellent candidate.

### YOU SHOULD NOW KNOW:

- What the application you are going to build does
- What the application will roughly look like
- What the data for the application will look like
- What the architecture of the application will consist of

# CHAPTER 8

# Introduction to MongoDB

The application you are about to build needs a way to store and serve data. Before you dive into writing your Dart application, let's review some high-level concepts about working with databases. In this chapter, you'll learn about the document-oriented database MongoDB, and how to interact with it.

# RELATIONAL VS. NOSQL DATABASES

When picking a database for a new project, you have two primary types of technology choices:

- **Relational databases**, represented by offerings such as Oracle, MySQL, and Postgres.
- **Non-relational databases**, sometimes referred to as NoSQL solutions, are represented by offerings such as MongoDB, Cassandra, Redis, and many others.

Although feature sets can vary greatly between implementations, the primary difference between relational and non-relational databases is in the way they enforce rules around how users structure their data.

*Relational databases* attempt to model relationships across an application domain by isolating the different facets of the domain into unique groupings known as tables. Tables must be defined prior to any data being written to the database.

A table is a collection of *properties*, which are represented by *columns*, and *entities*, which are represented by *rows*:

- **Row:** A row is an instance of an entity that contains multiple values; each value corresponds to one of the table's columns.
- **Column:** A column describes a specific property of the entity.
- **Table:** A table ensures that all the entities inside of it have the same properties, thus ensuring that the entities are uniform and of the same type.

The collection of tables inside a database, and the associated properties that define each table, are together referred to as a *database schema*.

*Non-relational databases* take a different approach to how they structure data. Although relational databases require you to define a schema up front, non-relational databases do not. Instead, each unit of data has a structure that is defined by the client at the time when the data is being inserted. This can lead to a more fluid approach to database design because entities in the same collection can store different types of data.

NoSQL and relational databases each have pros and cons, and each have capabilities to ensure speed, scale, and consistency. The data from Chapter 7 is actually modeled in a way that would work nicely with a traditional relational database. Despite this, we're going to go with a NoSQL database named MongoDB to define our data structures in Dart. Thanks to the flexibility of a non-relational approach, it's up to the client how to structure the data. Using MongoDB allows you to focus most of your energy on coding in Dart. The data structures will be defined in Dart instead of fussing with the ins and outs of managing relational-database schemas.

# WHY NOT DATABASE X?

The Dart community has provided support for many different kinds of relational and non-relational databases. For most projects, you have to make an architectural choice and live with it. We're going to rely heavily on MongoDB throughout the rest of the book. Doing so gives us a single unified approach that allows us to focus on solving development challenges as if they existed in the real world. However, you can easily modify many of the concepts and best practices you'll see in the following chapters to work with a different database.

For further reading, here are a few resources:

- https://pub.dartlang.org/packages/postgresql
- https://pub.dartlang.org/packages/sqljocky
- https://pub.dartlang.org/packages/dartabase
- https://pub.dartlang.org/packages/redis
- https://pub.dartlang.org/packages/memcache
- https://pub.dartlang.org/packages/neo4j_dart

# WHAT IS MONGODB?

Released in 2009, MongoDB is an open-source NoSQL database. MongoDB Inc., the creator of MongoDB, continues to act as its public steward and makes numerous contributions to the public code base. Since MongoDB is open source, Mongo Inc. profits solely from support service contracts rather than traditional commercial licensing fees. MongoDB has experienced massive public adoption, with high-profile clients such as ADP, the *New York Times*, Craigslist, and many more. You can find MongoDB support via many of the top hosting providers, such as Amazon Web Services, Heroku, Azure, and Google Cloud.

Mongo is a document-store style NoSQL database. *Document-store* means that within Mongo, each unique entity is a self-structuring document. At a low level, documents are a JSON derivative known as BSON, or Binary JSON. BSON allows JSON to provide a structure for the data, while later allowing conversion to a highly performant, compact data structure to store in memory and on disk.

JSON offers a concise, flexible format to structure and nest complex objects. JSON's self-defining structure is the foundation for MongoDB's query language, which allows MongoDB to sort, filter, and otherwise traverse the collections of documents in the database.

# INSTALLING MONGODB

Let's walk through how to acquire MongoDB for your specific operating system. In the following examples, we'll be working with version 3.0.4, which, at the time of this writing, is the most recent release. Here's how to grab the files for your machine.

## MAC OS X

For OS X, you'll be installing the binaries for your machine using the Terminal.

1. Open Terminal, and execute the following command lines to download the compressed files:

   ```
   $ cd ~
   $ curl -O https://fastdl.mongodb.org/osx/mongodb-osx-x86_64-3.0.4.tgz
   ```

2. Uncompress the downloaded files.

   ```
   $ tar -zxvf mongodb-osx-x86_64-3.0.4.tgz
   ```

3. Create a folder where MongoDB will store the data for the database.

   ```
   $ mkdir -p /data/db
   ```

4. Apply the proper user execution permissions to the data directory.

   ```
   $ sudo chown -R $USER /data/db/
   ```

5. Add the extracted folders to your execution path.

   ```
   $ printf "\n/Users/USER_HOME/mongodb-osx-x86_64-3.0.4/bin" |
   → sudo tee -a /etc/paths
   ```

6. Launch the Mongo daemon as a background task.

   ```
   $ mongod &
   ```

The Mongo daemon is the database process, and it listens for a connection on port 27017. By adding the extracted bin folder to your execution path, you've made available a database client named mongo, and a database daemon named mongod. When you launch MongoDB, you should see the Mongo database daemon output some start-up logs and then background itself. The Mongo database is now capable of accepting a connection from a Mongo client.

## WINDOWS

For Windows, the application files are available as a Microsoft installer (MSI).

1. Open your web browser and navigate to https://www.mongodb.org/downloads.
2. Click the Windows tab.
3. Select your version of Windows from the drop-down list.
4. Click Download MSI.
5. Open the downloaded MSI. You are greeted by a splash page. Click Next.
6. Select the Accept the License Agreement check box. Click Next.
7. Click Complete to install all the Mongo binaries to `C:\Program Files\MongoDB\Server\3.0\bin`.
8. Click Install, and wait for the wizard to complete.
9. Click Finish to exit the installer.

   The binaries are now installed.
10. Open Command Prompt or Power Shell.
11. Create a folder to use for the database data by issuing the following command:

    `md \data\db`

    Next, you'll be adding the `bin` folder to your environment path.
12. In the Windows search bar, locate Advanced System Settings.
13. Click the Environment Variables button.
14. Append the following new semicolon-delimited value to the end of the existing string:

    `;%PROGRAMFILES%\MongoDB\Server\3.0\bin\`
15. Restart Windows.
16. Open a new command-line session, and execute the following code in the command prompt:

    `mongod --version`

    The following line displays:

    `db version v3.0.4`
17. Execute the following line to start the Mongo daemon:

    `mongod`
18. Leave the Command Prompt dialog.

   The Mongo daemon is the database process, and it listens for a connection on port 27017. By adding the extracted `bin` folder to your execution path, you've made available a database client named `mongo` and a database daemon named `mongod`. When you launch Mongo, you should see the Mongo database daemon output some startup logs and then background itself. The Mongo database is now capable of accepting a connection from a Mongo client. This approach requires you to keep the command prompt open; otherwise, the `mongod` process will exit.

# THE MONGO CLIENT

You should now have all the Mongo binaries available via your system's environment path. Next, you will create a sample database and execute some basic CRUD (create, read, update, delete) interactions.

1. Start the Mongo command-line client.
2. Open a terminal, and execute the following command:

```
$ mongo

>
```

You are now dropped into the Mongo command-line interface, indicated by the > symbol.

## INTERACTING WITH A MONGO DATABASE

In Mongo, a database is the parent container for a series of collections. Each database gets a unique file on the file system, where all subsequent collection data is stored. To see the available database, execute the following:

```
>show dbs;
local                   0.078GB
```

This command shows a list of all the available databases in your /data/db folder. By default, mongo instantiates with a single database instance: local. Let's create your first custom database and then re-inspect the output of the previous command. To create a new database, issue the use command with a named value:

```
> use SampleDatabase;
switched to db SampleDatabase
> show dbs;
local                   0.078GB
```

### CREATING

As you can see from the response from the previous code, you've switched into SampleDatabase, but your new database doesn't exist yet. You need to store some data in it before it gets written to disk. Let's store your first document inside your first collection.

1. Run the following code:

```
> db.FoodCollection.insert({fruit: "Apple"})
WriteResult({ "nInserted" : 1 })
```

Let's take a look at what happened:

- From within the MongoDB client, the reference to the current database in use is db. In this case, db refers to the SampleDatabase that you created in the previous step. The db object is a container for your collections.

- You used dot notation off of the db object to access a yet to be created collection named FoodCollection. Once the collection is defined, the collection object exposes an API that allows you to interact with collection documents and the collection itself.

- You invoked the insert() function. The insert() function accepts a JSON object as an argument, which will be stored as our first document. The response from the database is a confirmation object verifying that 1 object was inserted.

2. Insert a second document into the FoodCollection:

```
> db.FoodCollection.insert({vegetable: "Lettuce"})
WriteResult({ "nInserted" : 1 })
```

In the second entry, notice that you introduce a new type of data. This new type of data has a field name of vegetable. This document can sit in the same collection as the previous document, which contains a document containing fruit. You can do this because of the schema-less nature of a non-relational database. Your collection is a list of JSON documents in which each supports its own data structure.

3. Insert a third document into the FoodCollection that will contain both fields:

```
> db.FoodCollection.insert({vegetable: "Lettuce", fruit: "Apple"})
WriteResult({ "nInserted" : 1 })
```

## READING

Let's take a look at what you stored.

1. Query the previously stored documents from your FoodCollection:

```
> db.FoodCollection.find()
{ "_id" : ObjectId("55951b6a39d3802d052f3038"), "vegetable" : "Lettuce",
→ "fruit" : "Apple" }
{ "_id" : ObjectId("55951b7439d3802d052f3039"), "fruit" : "Apple" }
{ "_id" : ObjectId("55951b7a39d3802d052f303a"), "vegetable" : "Lettuce" }
```

By invoking find() on the named collection and passing no arguments, you are asking the collection to return any document that the collection might contain.

As you can see, the collection returns the three documents you created, each with their defined document fields. Notice that MongoDB has automatically inserted an additional field, named _id. The _id is a unique hash generated for any document inserted into a database. It can be overwritten if needed.

2. Retrieve a list of objects by passing in a query object:

```
> db.FoodCollection.find({fruit : "Apple"})
{ "_id" : ObjectId("55951b6a39d3802d052f3038"), "vegetable" : "Lettuce",
→ "fruit" : "Apple" }
{ "_id" : ObjectId("55951b7439d3802d052f3039"), "fruit" : "Apple" }
```

By calling find() on the named collection and passing in a document with a key–value pair, you are asking the collection to return any document that contains the matching pair. The response includes the document with a single field and the document with both the vegetable field and the fruit field.

3. Expand your query object to match multiple properties:

```
> db.FoodCollection.find({"vegetable" : "Lettuce", "fruit" : "Apple"})
{ "_id" : ObjectId("55951b6a39d3802d052f3038"), "vegetable" : "Lettuce",
↪ "fruit" : "Apple" }
```

4. Using the _id from the previous response *(your local value will differ)*, query a collection by using the generated _id:

```
> db.FoodCollection.find({_id: ObjectId("55951b6a39d3802d052f3038")})
{ "_id" : ObjectId("55951b6a39d3802d052f3038"), "vegetable" : "Lettuce",
↪ "fruit" : "Apple" }
```

Collections allow you to create logical grouping between different types of data. Let's introduce some unrelated data about sports.

5. Run the following to add some sports data:

```
> db.BaseballStats.insert([{rbi: 12, name: "Doe"}, {rbi: 6, name: "Yates"}])
BulkWriteResult({ "nInserted" : 2 ... })
```

In this example, you're doing a couple of things worth noting:

- You are still using the same SampleDatabase, but you are again creating a new collection of data, this time named BaseballStats. Because baseball statistics have no direct relationship to your previous collection of FoodCollection, it's a good candidate for a new collection.

- You are again invoking the insert() function on the new collection. This time, you are passing in an array of documents. Note the wrapping square brackets [ ] and comma-separated values. This creates the new collection containing two documents.

### UPDATING

You can change the content of your document by using the update() function. The update() function accepts two arguments. The first argument is the query object, like you've been using. The second argument is a $set object with a nested-value object.

The parent object containing the $set field tells Mongo that you want to update a specific field and not just replace the object with a new document. Let's take a look at using update() with and without the $set field.

```
> db.BaseballStats.find()
{ "_id" : ObjectId("55952708d236b3558ff9f7b8"), "rbi" : 12, "name" : "Doe" }
{ "_id" : ObjectId("55952708d236b3558ff9f7b9"), "rbi" : 6, "name" : "Yates" }
> db.BaseballStats.update({rbi: 6}, {$set: {rbi: 7} })
WriteResult(...)
> db.BaseballStats.find()
{ "_id" : ObjectId("55952708d236b3558ff9f7b8"), "rbi" : 12, "name" : "Doe"}
{ "_id" : ObjectId("55952708d236b3558ff9f7b9"), "rbi" : 7, "name" : "Yates"}
```

By leveraging $set, you've changed the value of rbi from 6 to 7 without impacting the rest of the document. Let's issue an update() without using $set:

```
> db.BaseballStats.update({rbi: 7}, {rbi: 8})
WriteResult(...)
> db.BaseballStats.find()
{ "_id" : ObjectId("55952708d236b3558ff9f7b8"), "rbi" : 12, "name" : "Doe"}
{ "_id" : ObjectId("55952708d236b3558ff9f7b9"), "rbi" : 8 }
```

As you can see, after the second update, the field–value pair of "name" : "Yates" no longer exists. Omitting the $set object caused the supplied document to completely replace the matched document.

### DELETING
You can drop an entire collection and all its documents by invoking the drop() method on the collection reference.

```
> db.BaseballStats.drop()
True
> db.BaseballStats.find()
>
```

You can delete a document from a collection by invoking the remove() function. The remove() function takes two arguments: a query object and object containing a justOne Boolean field.

Omitting the justOne object tells Mongo to remove all documents that match the query object. If justOne is provided, the first matching element is removed. Let's create some data and then remove it using both approaches.

```
> db.BaseballStats.insert([{hits: 10, name: "Doe"},{hits: 11, name:
→ "Doe"},{hits: 12, name: "Doe"},{hits: 13, name: "Doe"}])
BulkWriteResult({ "nInserted" : 4})
> db.BaseballStats.find()
{ "_id" : ObjectId("55953000d236b3558ff9f7c4"), "hits" : 10, "name" : "Doe" }
{ "_id" : ObjectId("55953000d236b3558ff9f7c5"), "hits" : 11, "name" : "Doe" }
{ "_id" : ObjectId("55953000d236b3558ff9f7c6"), "hits" : 12, "name" : "Doe" }
{ "_id" : ObjectId("55953000d236b3558ff9f7c7"), "hits" : 13, "name" : "Doe" }

> db.BaseballStats.remove({name: "Doe"}, {justOne: true})
WriteResult({ "nRemoved" : 1 })
> db.BaseballStats.find({name: "Doe"})
{ "_id" : ObjectId("55953000d236b3558ff9f7c5"), "hits" : 11, "name" : "Doe" }
{ "_id" : ObjectId("55953000d236b3558ff9f7c6"), "hits" : 12, "name" : "Doe" }
{ "_id" : ObjectId("55953000d236b3558ff9f7c7"), "hits" : 13, "name" : "Doe" }
```

```
> db.BaseballStats.remove({name: "Doe"})
WriteResult({ "nRemoved" : 3 })
> db.BaseballStats.find({name: "Doe"})
>
```

In this example you're doing a couple of things worth noting:

- You `insert()` a list of documents with varying values for field hits, all of which have a value of "Doe" for the name. You follow that with a `find()` command to ensure that the data was written properly.
- You execute the function `remove()`, filtering for the name "Doe". To ensure that only the first item found is removed, you supply a config option Boolean of `justOne`.
- You then execute the `find()` command and notice that the document where the `hits` field is equal to 10 has been removed.
- You execute the function `remove()`, filtering for the name "Doe". This time you omit the `justOne` config option. You then execute the `find()` command and notice that all documents with a `name` field matching "Doe" have been removed from the collection.

## EMBEDDING DOCUMENTS

One of the powerful features of MongoDB is the ability to embed documents. Collections are a great way to create logical groupings, but those separations mean you can't execute a single query to get data from both collections; you have to issue two separate queries. For a lot of applications, that is perfectly acceptable. However, in cases where performance is a top priority, Mongo offers the capacity to embed documents inside documents.

Embedding allows you to nest objects inside objects. This is a familiar practice to anyone who's worked with JSON data structures.

Let's update the collection to use some embedded documents to track game states for each player. First, let's drop the collection so you can clean up the data. Dropping a collection removes all the documents from a collection.

1. Run the `drop()` and `find()` functions:

```
> db.BaseballStats.drop()
true
> db.BaseballStats.find()
>
```

Let's take a look at the JSON structure of the documents you are going to insert.

```
[
  {
    "name": "Doe",
    "games": [
      {
        "date": "06-22-2015",
```

```
          "at_bats": 3,
          "hits": 1
        },
        {
          "date": "06-23-2015",
          "at_bats": 3,
          "hits": 1
        },
        {
          "date": "06-23-2015",
          "at_bats": 3,
          "hits": 1
        }
      ]
    },
    {
      "name": "Yates",
      "games": [
        {
          "date": "06-22-2015",
          "at_bats": 4,
          "hits": 2
        },
        {
          "date": "06-23-2015",
          "at_bats": 2,
          "hits": 0
        },
        {
          "date": "06-23-2015",
          "at_bats": 4,
          "hits": 4
        }
      ]
    }
]
```

Next, you will insert the above JSON code into your collection. Luckily, the Mongo client supports multiline entries.

2. Construct the opening line of the query, and press Return/Enter.

```
> db.BaseballStats.insert(
...
```

You can manually begin entering the JSON code, or you can paste it directly into the command prompt.

3. Enter each new line as needed by pressing the Return/Enter key.

MongoDB understands that you are creating a document. It will wait for the JSON structure to be closed before executing.

4. When you're finished placing the JSON structure into the MongoDB client, append an additional closing parenthesis, and press Return/Enter.

```
... )
```

If you entered the JSON code correctly, Mongo created two new documents for you. Each document contains a field named games that will be an array of nested documents.

5. Run a find() command to take a look at how Mongo has stored your data:

```
> db.BaseballStats.find()
{ "_id" : ObjectId("55953c05a9e58e4c4304eadb"), "name" : "Doe", "games" :
→ [ { "date" : "06-22-2015", "at_bats" : 3, "hits" : 1 }, { "date" :
→ "06-23-2015", "at_bats" : 3, "hits" : 1 }, { "date" : "06-23-2015",
→ "at_bats" : 3, "hits" : 1 } ] }
{ "_id" : ObjectId("55953c05a9e58e4c4304eadc"), "name" : "Yates", "games" :
→ [ { "date" : "06-22-2015", "at_bats" : 4, "hits" : 2 }, { "date" :
→ "06-23-2015", "at_bats" : 2, "hits" : 0 }, { "date" : "06-23-2015",
→ "at_bats" : 4, "hits" : 4 } ] }
```

6. Query a top-level object using the established query convention:

```
> db.BaseballStats.find({name: "Doe"})
{ "_id" : ObjectId("55953c05a9e58e4c4304eadb"), "name" : "Doe", "games" :
→ [ { "date" : "06-22-2015", "at_bats" : 3, "hits" : 1 }, { "date" :
→ "06-23-2015", "at_bats" : 3, "hits" : 1 }, { "date" : "06-23-2015",
→ "at_bats" : 3, "hits" : 1 } ] }
```

7. Ask the question "which players had a game with four hits?" by constructing the following query. It will return the entire root object.

```
> db.BaseballStats.find({"games.hits": 4})
{ "_id" : ObjectId("55953c05a9e58e4c4304eadc"), "name" : "Yates", "games" :
→ [ { "date" : "06-22-2015", "at_bats" : 4, "hits" : 2 }, { "date" :
→ "06-23-2015", "at_bats" : 2, "hits" : 0 }, { "date" : "06-23-2015",
→ "at_bats" : 4, "hits" : 4 } ] }
```

# SUMMARY

Congratulations, you've run through the basics of interacting with MongoDB. This is not intended to be a complete overview of how to use MongoDB. This chapter was designed to get you up and running quickly with a powerful, scalable database and to teach you the basic functionality that you will need to build your Just-In-Time Airlines ticketing system.

## YOU SHOULD NOW KNOW:

- What a relational database is
- What a non-relational database is
- What the high-level differences are between a relational and non-relational database
- How to acquire and install MongoDB for your operating system
- What the MongoDB daemon is
- What the MongoDB client is
- How to create, read, update, and delete documents from a collection
- What a collection is
- What a document is
- How to query and retrieve a document based on a matched subdocument
- How to embed a document in a document

CHAPTER 9

# Mongo Dart

In the previous chapter, you learned the basics of working with MongoDB. By using MongoDB, you are leveraging a powerful database that facilitates a client-centric approach to structuring data. It's now time to use Dart to populate the seed data that will power the Just-In-Time Airlines ticketing application.

# SETTING UP YOUR PROJECT

In this chapter, you'll learn how to use the MongoDB Dart client. You'll query and write data to your MongoDB using the community package `mongo_dart`. Next, you will download the seed data corresponding to the data structures outlined in Chapter 7. Finally, you'll write that data to MongoDB.

Let's start by setting up the project for you new ticketing application. You'll be using the `tickets` project folder for the remainder of the book.

1.  Navigate to the `~/projects/` folder on your operating system.
2.  Create a new folder, named `tickets`.
3.  Open the IDEA Editor.
4.  Select Open either from the splash screen or from under the File menu.
5.  In the dialog, navigate to the `~/projects/` folder.
6.  Highlight the `tickets` folder, and click Choose to select it.

    This will import your `tickets` project folder into IDEA. Next, you'll create some folders inside your `tickets` project folder.

7.  On the left side of the editor in the IDE's Project panel, Control-click the `tickets` folder, and choose New > Directory. Name the new directory `bin`.
8.  Create another directory inside your `tickets` folder, and name it `lib`.
9.  On the left side of the editor in the IDE's Project panel, Control-click the `tickets` folder, and choose New > File. Name the new file `pubspec.yaml`.

    This should look familiar if you've followed along since Part 1. Let's add a new folder that will be used only by your package.

10. Navigate into the `tickets` folder on the left side of the editor. This time create a directory inside your `lib` folder, and name it `db`.
11. Control-click the db folder, and choose New > File. Name the new file `db_config.dart`.
12. Control-click the db folder, and choose New > File. Name the new file `seeder.dart`.

    I used a plugin named Export JSON to convert the Google Sheets from Chapter 7 into a JSON file for consumption by Dart.

13. Use your preferred method of choice to download the file at `http://bit.ly/dart_seed_json`.
14. Name the downloaded file `seed.json`, and place it in your `/lib/db/` folder.

    The resulting directory structure should look like **Figure 9.1**.

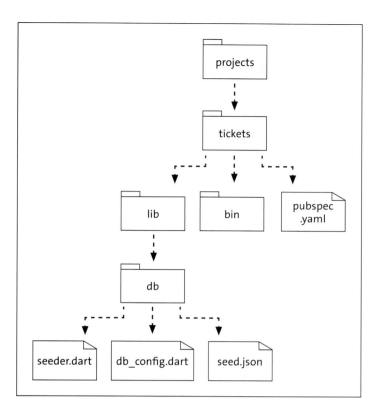

**FIGURE 9.1** Directory structure

# DOWNLOADING AND INSTALLING MONGO DART PACKAGES

Next, you will download the required database dependencies. You'll be introducing more dependencies as your application grows, but for now you're just focusing on working with MongoDB. You'll be using the community package named mongo_dart. The mongo_dart package is a server-side library that provides Dart with a back-end client to connect to a MongoDB database server. Although not supported directly by Google, it has a long project history, and is used by many popular Dart frameworks. More information about mongo_dart is available at https://pub.dartlang.org/packages/mongo_dart.

To install `mongo_dart`, you'll be using Pub to download and manage the dependencies. Let's go ahead and set up the `pubspec.yaml` file.

1. Open `pubspec.yaml`, and enter the following:

```
name: tickets
version: 0.0.1
description: A ticket commerce application
author: <your_username> <your_email>
homepage: <your_url>
environment:
  sdk: '>=1.0.0 <2.0.0'
dependencies:
  json_object: "1.0.19"
  mongo_dart: "0.1.46"
```

The concept of a `pubspec.yaml` file should be familiar to you from Chapter 5. In short, you're defining the package name of your application as `tickets` and assigning some meta information about you, the project author. You are then telling the project that it must use a Dart SDK version greater than or equal to version 1.0.0 but less than version 2.0.0. Finally, you are requiring two dependencies to be exposed to the parent application: `json_object` and `mongo_dart`. You'll be using the functionality from `json_object` to convert JSON string values into a Dart JSON object that can then be inserted into MongoDB.

2. Once your `pubspec.yaml` file is generated, click the Get Dependencies link in the upper-right corner of IDEA. This executes the pub get command for your project and downloads the needed dependencies. You should see something similar to the following output:

```
Working dir: /Users/jmurphy/projects/tickets
/Users/jmurphy/dart-sdk/bin/pub get
Resolving dependencies...
Got dependencies!

...
Process finished with exit code 0
```

## VERSION NUMBERS

Although many folks love to run the latest and greatest, I highly suggest using the version numbers that are listed throughout the book. The Pub repositories store all the various versions for years to come, so they'll remain available long after this book has been published. By requesting a package in `pubspec.yaml` with a specific version number, Pub will install that exact requested version from its repositories. The benefit of using the exact version listed in the book is that I can guarantee they'll work together as described. Once you've finished the book, feel free to try to update the versions to their latest distributions.

# EXPOSING DATABASE CREDENTIALS

You need to ensure that you are using the same credentials to access your database across your entire application. Let's go ahead and create a simple class that exposes the credentials in a consistent manner. (Note that the package containing class Resource will change with Dart 1.14.0.) Open your lib/db/db_config.dart file:

```
class DbConfigValues {
  String dbName = 'Tickets';
  String dbURI = 'mongodb://127.0.0.1/';
  Resource dbSeed = const Resource('package:tickets/db/seed.json');
  int dbSize = 10;

  String get testDbName => dbName + "-test";
  String get testDbURI => dbURI;
  Resource get testDbSeed => dbSeed;
  int get testDbSize => dbSize;
}
```

This will serve you over the next couple of chapters to ensure that you are always providing the same credentials to your MongoDB. This class also exposes getters to return credentials that will allow you to spin up a test database once you start writing unit tests.

# SEEDING DATA IN DART

Now that your project has the required dependencies installed, you're ready to start writing the seeder. Seeder is a utility that helps install the needed data for the primary application. Let's take a look at the conversion process from a Google Sheet to JSON to a MongoDB collection.

## COLLECTIONS

Each sheet in the workbook is represented as a top-level property in the JSON file.

```
{
  "Routes": [...],
  "Times": [...],
  "Cities" [...],
  "Bookings": [...],
  "Transactions": [...]
}
```

Each of these top-level properties will represent a collection in MongoDB.

**FIGURE 9.2**
Sheet representation

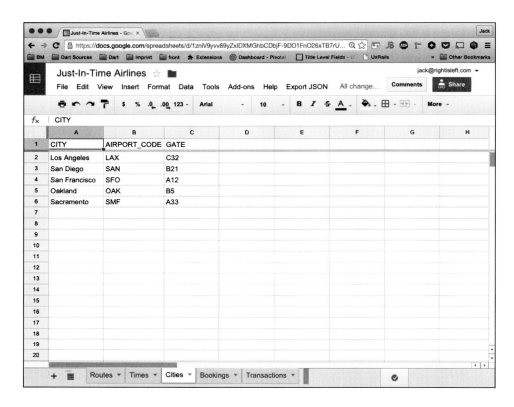

## DOCUMENTS

Each row from the Google Sheet is represented as a property in the downloaded JSON file and will eventually become a document in MongoDB. Each document will exist as part of a collection in which the document fields and values are assigned by items with corresponding column labels and values from the Google Sheet. Look at the example in **Figure 9.2**.

The sheet from Figure 9.2 has the JSON representation in the seed.json file (**Example 9.1**):

**EXAMPLE 9.1**

```
{
  "Cities": [
    {
      "city": "Los Angeles",
      "airportcode": "LAX",
      "gate": "C32"
    },
    {
      "city": "San Diego",
```

```
        "airportcode": "SAN",
        "gate": "B21"
    },
    {
        "city": "San Francisco",
        "airportcode": "SFO",
        "gate": "A12"
    },
    {
        "city": "Oakland",
        "airportcode": "OAK",
        "gate": "B5"
    },
    {
        "city": "Sacramento",
        "airportcode": "SMF",
        "gate": "A33"
    }
  ]
}
```

The sheet name corresponds to the collection name, which is represented by the top-level JSON property of Cities. The columns from the Cities sheet—city, airportcode, and gate—are represented as the properties on each of the child JSON objects.

Finally, rows from the sheet are represented as an array of objects whose properties have been assigned the values from their respective row.

# READING A FILE FROM THE FILE SYSTEM

Now you're going to build a stand-alone command-line application that reads in the seed.json file. You'll be leveraging two of Dart's built-in packages: dart:io and dart:async.

- dart:io is a built-in Dart library that allows you to interact with files, directories, processes, HTTP servers, and numerous other system-level features. dart:io is restricted purely to command-line applications and cannot be leveraged by browser implementations.

- dart:async is a built-in Dart library that allows you to leverage many of the asynchronous features found in Dart. For a review on asynchronous programming, please refer to Chapter 6.

Because this is a stand-alone command-line application, you'll be implementing the `main()` interface in seeder.dart. This will enable seeder.dart to act as an application entry point.

1. Open the seeder.dart file and enter the code from **Example 9.2**:

   **EXAMPLE 9.2**

   ```dart
   import 'dart:io';
   import 'dart:async';
   import 'db_config.dart';

   main() {
     DbConfigValues config = new DbConfigValues();
     var importer = new Seeder(config.dbName, config.dbURI, config.dbSeed);
     importer.readFile();
   }

   class Seeder {
     final String _dbURI;
     final String _dbName;
     final Resource _dbSeedFile;

     Seeder(String this._dbName, String this._dbURI, Resource
     this._dbSeedFile);

     Future readFile() {
       return _dbSeedFile.readAsString().then( (String item) => print(item) );
     }
   }
   ```

2. Run the seeder.dart file.

   You should see the contents of the seed.json file printed to the output window. Let's take a look at what you just did.

   - By implementing the function `main()`, you've given Dart a root execution context for the utility application.

   - Inside `main()` you instantiated an instance of class Seeder. Seeder's parameterized constructor accepts a Resource argument that corresponds to the asset location of the JSON file using package syntax. These values are exposed from your class DBConfigValues.

   - Resource is a class exposed by dart:core. It allows the asynchronous loading of assets at runtime, its constructor uses the same package locator syntax found throughout the rest of your library, and helps developers avoid using relative paths.

- You declared a class named Seeder. Seeder has one function, named readFile(), that returns an instance of the future.
- You then executed the asynchronous function named readAsString() to make a request to the file system to retrieve the contents of the seed.json file. The function readAsString() returns a future with a value containing the raw JSON string.
- Using the futures pattern, you passed in a function expression to the then() completer method. This method waits until the future completes (the asset finishes loading), then executes the function expression. The function expression prints the returned string value to the console.

## CONVERTING TO JSON

In Example 9.2, you were able to access the string value of the seed.json file. Right now the value is a single string. In order to get access to each of the elements, you need to convert the string value into a JSON object. To handle this conversion, you'll be leveraging the package json_object.

The JsonObject class is a wrapper for dart:convert encode and decode functionality. It will deserialize a JSON string into a Dart Map object and then expose the map properties using dot notation.

Because you don't have a concrete Dart class that maps to the data structure of the seed.json file, JsonObject leverages the NoSuchMethod functionality to implement dot notation field access. In short, when calling a field using dot notation, JsonObject will trap the NoSuchMethod error and use its contents to discern a key that can then be used to access the instance from the internal map representation of the data structure. The end result is an instance that mimics "dynamic programming" practices, in which properties are not necessarily defined or expected at author time.

Although this is good for quick conversions, we'll be looking at a more Dart-idiomatic approach later in the book: Dartson.

In **Example 9.3**, you'll be using future chaining to ensure the order of operations on the conversion.

1. Update the seeder.dart file to the following:

**EXAMPLE 9.3**
```dart
import 'dart:io';
import 'dart:async';
import 'package:json_object/json_object.dart';
import 'db_config.dart';


main() {
```

```
      DbConfigValues config = new DbConfigValues();
      var importer = new Seeder(config.dbName, config.dbURI, config.dbSeed);
      importer.readFile();
    }

    class Seeder {
      final String _dbURI;
      final String _dbName;
      final Resource _dbSeedFile;

      Seeder(String this._dbName, String this._dbURI, Resource this._dbSeedFile);

      Future readFile() {
         return _dbSeedFile.readAsString()
        .then((String item) => new JsonObject.fromJsonString(item))
        .then(printJson);
      }

    JsonObject printJson(JsonObject json) {
        json.keys.forEach((String collectionKey) {
          print('Collections Name: ' + collectionKey);
          var collection = json[collectionKey];
          print('Collection: ' + collection.toString());
          collection.forEach((document) {
            print('Document: ' + document.toString());
          });
        });
        return json;
      }
    }
```

Let's review what you did in Example 9.3:

- You used a function expression to deserialize the string item from a single large string entity into a JSON object. The function expression then returns the new JsonObject instance to the future.

- You introduced a new function, named printJson(), that will be used to chain together multiple asynchronous futures. It expects the argument passed to it to be of type JsonObject. By having previously converted the parameter to a JSON object, you were able to treat the instance as a map.

The Map object exposed a property named keys, which exposed each of the keys in a map via an iterator. The top-level keys in the JSON object correspond to the top-level objects names from the previous section. You then iterated over the keys and printed the collection name, followed by the respective document keyed on the respective collection name.

- Because each collection is a list of documents, you individually grabbed each list, and you iterated over the members of the list using the forEach() method. As a result, you printed each row from the sheet. Each row will eventually represent a document in MongoDB and contain each of its unique properties and values.

- Because this is just printing out the data structure, you returned the unmodified JsonObject instance to the future. This allows the next element in the chain to accept the instance as a parameter.

2. Run seeder.dart again.

In the output window, you should see the JSON object broken into the representation that you're going to put into the database.

```
Observatory listening on http://127.0.0.1:63193
Collections Name: Routes
Collection: {"route":"SAN_LAX","duration":45,"price1":29... ... ... ...
Document: {"route":"SAN_SFO","duration":140,"price1":49,"price2":79,
→ "price3":99,"seats":7}
Document: {"route":"SAN_OAK","duration":150,"price1":49,"price2":79,
→ "price3":99,"seats":7}
//...
```

# CONNECTING TO MONGO FROM DART

Next you'll write some actual data to MongoDB. Your project now has the required dependencies installed, and you've decoded your seed.json file, so you're ready to connect Dart to MongoDB.

1. Ensure that you've completed Chapter 8 and that the mongod process is still running.

2. Modify your seeder.dart file to match **Example 9.4**:

**EXAMPLE 9.4**

```
import 'dart:io';
import 'dart:async';
import 'package:json_object/json_object.dart';
import 'db_config.dart';
```

```dart
import 'package:mongo_dart/mongo_dart.dart';

main() {
  DbConfigValues config = new DbConfigValues();
  var importer = new Seeder(config.dbName, config.dbURI, config.dbSeed);
  importer.readFile();
}

class Seeder {
  final String _dbURI;
  final String _dbName;
  final Resource _dbSeedFile;

  Seeder(String this._dbName, String this._dbURI, Resource this._dbSeedFile);

  Future readFile() {
    return _dbSeedFile.readAsString()
    .then((String item) => new JsonObject.fromJsonString(item))
    .then(printJson)
    .then(insertJsonToMongo)
    .then(closeDatabase);
  }

  JsonObject printJson(JsonObject json) {
    json.keys.forEach((String collectionKey) {
      print('Collections Name: ' + collectionKey);
      var collection = json[collectionKey];
      print('Collection: ' + collection.toString());
      collection.forEach((document) {
        print('Document: ' + document.toString());
      });
    });
    return json;
  }

  Future<Db> insertJsonToMongo(JsonObject json) async
  {
    Db database = new Db(_dbURI + _dbName);
```

```
    await database.open();
    await Future.forEach(json.keys, (String collectionName) async {

      //grabs the collection instance
      DbCollection collection = new DbCollection(database, collectionName);

      //takes a list of maps and writes to a collection
      return collection.insertAll(json[collectionName]);
    });
    return database;
  }


  Future closeDatabase(Db database) {
    return database.close();
  }
}
```

Let's review what you did in Example 9.4:

- The constructor method signature for class Seeder is modified to require a string value of _dbName and _dbURI.

- _dbName tells mongo_dart which database within MongoDB to use. If it does not exist, it will be created. You'll be using a database with the name of Tickets to store all the data.

- _dbURI tells mongo_dart that the Mongo daemon is listening at IP 127.0.0.1, which is your local machine. If your database is on a different computer, you could modify the URI (uniform resource identifier) to point to a different location. Many other parameters can be supplied when initializing a connection to MongoDB. Please refer to the documentation for more information.

- Inside the insertJsonToMongo() function, you instantiated an instance of Db from the mongo_dart library. This instance is the primary interface for your interactions with the mongo_dart client.

- Upon instantiation, you haven't actually connected to the database yet. You need to initialize a new session by calling the open() method on the instanceof class Db.

    Many interactions with MongoDB are asynchronous because they require a round trip from the Dart client to the server and back. The mongo_dart library supports this by making heavy use of futures. The function open() is the first example of this. You used the await keyword from Dart to mimic a synchronous request. Once the open() future returns, the Db can accept commands and the execution context will continue.

- You again accessed the json.keys object property, which is a collection of the JSON property names, in order to traverse the JSON data structure. You have multiple asynchronous requests that are going to be made, so you wrapped the iterator in a future and again used the await keyword.

- You used the keys collection to acquire the list of map items representing each collection. By instantiating a new instance using new DbCollection(), you are telling MongoDB that you want a new collection that corresponds to the named value from the JSON data structure. The variable collection stores a reference to the new DbCollection instance. As you saw in Chapter 8 with the MongoDB client, a collection doesn't exist until it contains data.

- The mongo_dart library expects all documents to be of type Map. It can support single insertion, or it will accept a List<Map> for multiple items. The seed file has already been converted to a list of maps via JsonObject. Using collection.insertAll(), you can save all the entities for each collection in one call.

  In order to execute a single save action, you first acquire the whole collection by providing the collectionName key to the instance of JsonObject. That will return a List<Map> instance of the collection that you then provide as argument to the aforementioned insertAll() method.

- The last method in the chain is closeDatabase(). This function accepts an instance of Db. Every call to open() must have a corresponding call to close(). If you don't call close(), Dart will leave the MongoDB connection process running and cause a memory leak. We'll take a look at database pooling in future chapters.

3. Run seeder.dart again.

   In the output window, you should see the JsonObject output again, but the last line should read as follows:

   ```
   Process finished with exit code 0
   ```

## VERIFYING THE DATA

Now that your seed file has been inserted into MongoDB, let's make sure the data persisted correctly.

1. Open the terminal and use the command-line Mongo client to query some of the new data.

   ```
   $ mongo
   MongoDB shell version: 3.0.3
   connecting to: test
   > use Tickets
   switched to db Tickets
   ```

2. Now that you're in the Tickets database, let's see what collections are available:

   ```
   > show collections;
   Bookings
   Cities
   Routes
   ```

```
Times
Transactions
system.indexes
```

3. Check one of the collections to make sure it has the documents and the corresponding document values:

```
> db.Cities.find()
{ "_id" : ObjectId("559e9f1c48f62fcc6e14fe1e"), "city" : "Los Angeles",
→ "airportcode" : "LAX", "gate" : "C32" }
{ "_id" : ObjectId("559e9f1c48f62fcc6e14fe1f"), "city" : "San Diego",
→ "airportcode" : "SAN", "gate" : "B21" }
{ "_id" : ObjectId("559e9f1c48f62fcc6e14fe20"), "city" : "San Francisco",
→ "airportcode" : "SFO", "gate" : "A12" }
{ "_id" : ObjectId("559e9f1c48f62fcc6e14fe21"), "city" : "Oakland",
→ "airportcode" : "OAK", "gate" : "B5" }
{ "_id" : ObjectId("559e9f1c48f62fcc6e14fe22"), "city" : "Sacramento",
→ "airportcode" : "SMF", "gate" : "A33" }
```

# SUMMARY

Congratulations, you have now seeded your MongoDB with the data needed to power your ticketing application. We'll be working a lot more with the mongo_dart library, but you should now have a basic understanding of how to interact with MongoDB from dart.

## YOU SHOULD NOW KNOW:

- That your tickets project is set up for the remainder of the book
- That your pubspec.yaml is configured to pull down third-party packages
- That your seed data is accessible through a MongoDB
- How to connect Dart to MongoDB
- What a MongoDB Connection URI is
- How to read a file from the file system asynchronously
- How to deserialize a string into JSON
- How JsonObject enables dot notation, and its associated downsides
- How to work with an asynchronous DbCollection instance
- How to work with an asynchronous Db instance
- How to open a MongoDB session
- How to close a MongoDB session
- How to write a document from Dart to MongoDB

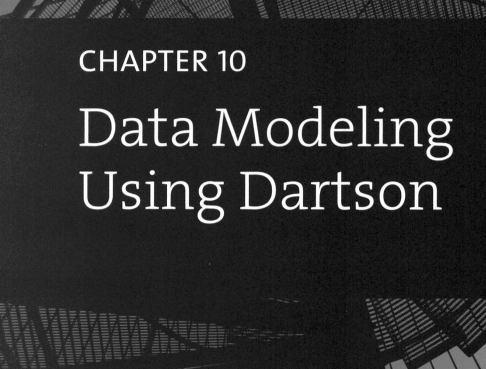

# CHAPTER 10

# Data Modeling Using Dartson

In this chapter, you will set up a `MongoModel` class that will expose basic CRUD (Create, Read, Update, and Delete) operations to your Mongo database. `MongoModel` will be your primary interface to the `mongo_dart` library. It's here that you'll implement database connection pooling and other MongoDB helper functionality. Later in this chapter, you'll be learning how to define an interface for each MongoDB document using a Dart class paired with Dartson for serialization. You will then share your data structures between your client code and server code. By the end of this chapter, you will have a solid understanding of how to handle data storage for your application.

# WHY DARTSON

Although a RESTful system enforces a standard method of interaction with a web server, it does not dictate which type of content your messages must be sent in. This has resulted in multiple media types being used for API design, including HTML, XML, JSON, Binary, and many others. As you may have guessed from previous chapters, you will be using JSON to send data between the client and server. You'll go one step further and leverage Dart's capacity to run on both server and client by sharing your data structure between both tiers.

JSON stands for JavaScript Object Notation and is one of the most popular interchange formats on the web. It is based on the popular ECMAScript 3 syntax and allows for easily readable object creation. It supports name–value pairs of strings, arrays, and objects—all of which combine to become the foundation for flexible hierarchical data structures.

The downside to working with JSON is that, like its JavaScript counterpart, it lacks strong typing. This represents a challenge to languages, like Dart, that provide rich, strongly typed data structures. To help you work effectively with JSON, we will introduce you to a serialization mechanism named Dartson.

Dartson is a community library that enables the serialization of JSON data to native Dart class instances and vice versa. This means that classes leveraging Dartson will retain full type integrity and IDE tooling. This stands in stark contrast to the approach used in Chapter 9, which, by using `JsonObject`, allowed Dart to serialize JSON data into a glorified dynamic object.

To successfully implement serialization, Dartson uses two different approaches, the first of which is reflection and the second of which is a transformer at build time. Dart ships with a core library dedicated to handling reflection: `dart:mirrors`.

Mirrors is a powerful library that enables the developer to observe and modify objects at run time. Mirrors are ideal for serialization tasks and work extremely well when run in the Dart VM. At a high level, reflection works by taking apart an object and traversing its structure node by node. In static languages, this works extremely effectively. This is definitely the case when running in the Dart VM.

Dart hits a stumbling block when working with reflection and the transformer dart2js. If you recall, the dart2js process takes native Dart code, inspects its structure, and outputs optimized JavaScript code. To ensure the output code is compact, dart2js takes only what parts of the Dart code base it needs to execute efficiently. Using a process known as tree shaking, dart2js is able to discard any unused or dead code. When reflection is used, there is simply too much surface area for dart2js to efficiently transpile, and the output becomes untenable.

The challenge with reflection is that dart2js can't distinguish between a reflection utility that inspects all the methods on a class and an object that, for example, might call only one of 100 methods from that same class. Reflection would cause the 99 unused methods to be marked as active.

In the previous case, using reflection in conjunction with dart2js would result in a massive exported JavaScript file. To bypass this limitation, Dartson ships with both a reflection-based implementation for back-end applications and a Dartson build-time transformer for applications that select JavaScript as a compilation target.

This approach makes Dartson the ideal solution for implementation serialization on entities that exist on both client and server.

## MONGO POOLING

In Chapter 9, you constructed a class named Seeder that leveraged the mongo_dart library, and you filled your database with the initial data needed for your ticketing application. You established a connection to MongoDB using the open() method, and when you were finished seeding data, you terminated the connection using the close() method. That approach works great for simple scripts, but it can become a performance bottleneck even for small applications.

To avoid the performance overhead of constantly opening and closing a connection to the database, we will implement a pattern known as *connection pooling*. Connection pooling allows an application to reallocate an open database connection to a new consumer if the previous consumer is finished with it.

A connection pool is, in short, a managed list of opened connections. When an application starts, it opens a specified number of open database connections and makes them available to anyone who requests an instance. All a connection pool asks is that when the consumer is finished with the connection, the connection is returned to the pool.

To use this technique and play by the rules, you will install a library named connection_pool. The Connection Pool library provides much of the logic for maintaining the pool of databases via a concise interface.

1. From the IDEA project panel, open pubspec.yaml, and add the following line of code under the dependencies section:

   connection_pool: "0.1.0+2"

2. Click Get Dependencies to download connection_pool to your packages folder. You should see the following output:

   Got dependencies!

3. From the IDEA project panel, Control-click the bin folder, select New > File, and name the file mongo_pool.dart.

   Next, you'll need to implement the abstract connection pool in a concrete class to enable a single instance of your pooling implementation to be managed.

4. Enter the code in **Example 10.1** into the mongo_pool.dart file:

   **EXAMPLE 10.1**

   ```
   import 'package:connection_pool/connection_pool.dart';
   import 'package:mongo_dart/mongo_dart.dart';
   ```

```
import 'dart:async';

class MongoDbPool extends ConnectionPool<Db> {

  String uri;

  MongoDbPool(String this.uri, int poolSize) : super(poolSize);

  //overrides method in ConnectionPool
  void closeConnection(Db conn) {
    conn.close();
  }

  //overrides method in ConnectionPool
  Future<Db> openNewConnection() {
    var conn = new Db(uri);
    return conn.open().then((_) => conn);
  }
}
```

Let's take a look at what you just did:

- You imported the required libraries. Having added connection_pool to the pubspec.yaml file, connection_pool is now available for consumption by your libraries. You have also exposed the mongo_dart library and the built-in Dart async library to your new class.

- You declared a class named MongoDbPool that extends ConnectionPool. ConnectionPool itself is an abstract class that accepts a generic type using the notation ConnectionPool<T>. By also providing a database class type upon extension, you can set the declared class as the database of choice. In your case, you expect the mongo_dart class of Db.

- You implemented class MongoDbPool. The class has a constructor method that accepts the URI of the MongoDB location. It also accepts a parameter of poolSize, which is the number of database connections that will be established on instantiation.

- You implemented the interface requirements of the async methods openNewConnection() and closeConnection(). These need to be implemented by the subclass; otherwise, the abstract ConnectionPool class is incomplete.

The ConnectionPool superclass leaves database connection instantiation up to the subclass. This gives the developer control over how database connections are opened and closed.

What you have now is a concrete implementation of the abstract class ConnectionPool and all the logic required to manage multiple instances of database connections. This ensures that if you have multiple requests to your back end occurring at the same time, you should have enough connections available to handle the load. Throughout the rest of the chapter, you'll be using this pooling instance in your MongoModel implementation.

# DARTSON SERIALIZATION

You're going to install a library named `dartson` that contains the code for both client and server execution. You'll then be constructing a shared library named `ticket_schemas` in which you'll define classes of data transfer objects (DTOs) for all the data structures in your MongoDB. DTOs encapsulate logical groupings of values related to a topic of interest. They can be passed around or across a network.

1. From the IDEA project panel, open `pubspec.yaml`, and add the following line of code under the dependencies section:

   ```
   dartson: "0.2.4"
   ```

2. At the end of your `pubspec.yaml` file, add a new top-level element named `transformers` by adding the following:

   ```
   transformers:
   - dartson
   ```

3. Click Get Dependencies to download `dartson` to your packages folder. You should see the following output:

   ```
   Got dependencies!
   ```

   By adding Dartson to your `pubspec.yaml` file, you have made Dartson available to your project and configured the transformer to run at build time. Your `pubspec.yaml` file should now resemble **Example 10.2**:

**EXAMPLE 10.2**

```
name: 'tickets'
version: 0.0.1
description: A ticket commerce application
author: Jack Murphy jack@rightisleft.com
homepage: https://www.rightisleft.com
environment:
  sdk: '>=1.0.0 <2.0.0'
dependencies:
  json_object: "1.0.19"
  mongo_dart: "0.1.46"
  connection_pool: "0.1.0+2"
  dartson: "0.2.4"
transformers:
- dartson
```

Next, you are going to set up a shared folder that will contain classes intended to be used by both the client and the server. This will isolate your shared code and ensure it can run correctly in both environments.

4. From the IDEA project panel, Control-click the `lib` folder, select New > Directory, and name the directory `shared`.

5. Control-click the `lib/shared` folder, select New > File, and name the file `schemas.dart`.

   This will be the parent library that will contain all your shared DTOs. You'll extend this later in the book to wrap your DTO classes in a list for additional functionality.

6. Control-click the `lib/shared` folder, select New > Directory, and name the directory `dtos`.

7. Control-click the `dtos` folder, select New > File, and name the file `base_dto.dart`.

   The `BaseDTO` class will be the abstract parent of all your DTOs.

8. Control-click the `dtos` folder, select New > File, and name the file `city_dto.dart`.

   This will be your first concrete implementation of a DTO.

9. Open the `base_dto.dart` file.

   As stated earlier, the `BaseDTO` class will be the abstract parent of all your DTOs. In this case, you'll be modeling your DTOs to match the data coming from MongoDB.

10. Implement your abstract class with the following:

```
part of ticket_schemas;

class BaseDTO
{
  String id;
  String collection_key;
}
```

**NOTE:** By default, the Dartson transformer knows only about Dart's native types. This book uses the unique String provided by `ObjectId`. To learn about custom Dartson transformers for use with third-party packages, check out https://github.com/eredo/dartson.

Let's take a look at what you just did:

- You declared that this class is part of the library named `ticket_schemas`. This indicates that the library is intended to be used in a parent library.

- You declared a class with a name of `BaseDTO`. This is the superclass that all your concrete implementations will inherit from.

- You declared that all instances of a `BaseDTO` class will have a minimum of two properties available. The first property `id` is a placeholder for each unique MongoDB ID. All objects coming from the database should have at least an `id`. The second property is the `collection_key`. You are modeling MongoDB documents, and all documents belong to a collection; this key is intended to pair a DTO with a collection in your MongoDB database. This is an important concept to understand when you're implementing CRUD actions later.

11. Implement your top-level library by opening the file schemas.dart and entering the following code:

```
library ticket_schemas;

import 'package:dartson/dartson.dart';

//Injectables
part 'dtos/base_dto.dart';
part 'dtos/city_dto.dart';
```

Let's take a look at what you just did:

- You declared a new library named ticket_schemas. This allows you to include a bi-directional pairing using the keywords part and part of.

- You imported the package dartson. Since this is a top-level library, Dartson and any other exposed libraries will be included in the inherited scope of the partials. You have now exposed Dartson to your DTOs.

- You paired two partial libraries using the keyword part. This loads the libraries into the ticket_schemas namespace.

Let's create your first concrete implementation of a BaseDTO.

12. Open the city_dto.dart file, and enter the following code:

```
part of ticket_schemas;

@Entity()
class CityDTO extends BaseDTO  {
  String collection_key = "Cities";
  String city;
  String airportcode;
  String gate;
}
```

Let's take a look at what you just did:

- You declared that this partial is part of the library named ticket_schemas. Even though you extended a class that is part of the same parent library, class extensions modify only the class object, and not the relationship between the partial file and its parent library.

- The Dartson library exposes a metadata annotation named @Entity. @Entity will add the following class declaration to Dartson's list of classes that will be eligible for JSON serialization functionality. In this case, @Entity registers the CityDTO class with Dartson.

- You modeled the data that you expect to come back from the Mongo document. The defined class fields map to the document fields you generated in the previous chapters. The only assignment you made is for the collection_key field, which is assigned a string value of its associated collection in MongoDB.

You'll continue the pattern of hard coding the DTO's collection_key so you can make a pairing between the class of DTO and the collection. This allows you to use a DTO class to query data from MongoDB without also needing to know which collection to target. With this pattern, you can create a Dart DTO first and then create your own collection in MongoDB. We'll look at this in more depth later in the chapter.

You need to repeat this pattern for each collection that was built in the previous chapter.

13. Create purchase_dto.dart inside the lib/shared/dtos folder, and enter the **Example 10.3** code:

**EXAMPLE 10.3**

```
part of ticket_schemas;

@Entity()
class PurchaseDTO extends BaseDTO
{
  String collection_key = "Purchases";

  //should be nums
  int flightID;
  int flightLevel;

  String ccn;
  String ccv;
  String bZip;

  String ccType;
  String ccExpiration;

  String pFirstName;
  String pMiddleName;
  String pLastName;
  String pEmail;

  String bFirstName;
  String bMiddleName;
  String bLastName;
  String bAddress;
  String bCity;
  String bState;
  String bCountry;
  String transactionId;
}
```

**14.** Create route_dto.dart inside the lib/shared/dtos folder, and enter the **Example 10.4** code:

**EXAMPLE 10.4**

```
part of ticket_schemas;

@Entity()
class RouteDTO extends BaseDTO {
  String collection_key = "Routes";

  String route;
  num duration;
  num price1;
  num price2;
  num price3;
  int seats;

  String getDepartureCity() {
    return route.split('_')[0];
  }

  String getArrivalCity() {
    return route.split('_')[1];
  }
}
```

**15.** Create time_dto.dart inside the lib/shared/dtos folder, and enter the **Example 10.5** code:

**EXAMPLE 10.5**

```
part of ticket_schemas;

@Entity()
class TimeDTO extends BaseDTO {
  String collection_key = "Times";

  int flight;
  String departure;
  String arrival;
  int takeoff;
  RouteDTO route;
}
```

**16.** Create `transaction_dto.dart` inside the `lib/shared/dtos` folder, and enter the **Example 10.6** code:

**EXAMPLE 10.6**

```
part of ticket_schemas;

@Entity()
class TransactionDTO extends BaseDTO {
  String collection_key = "Transactions";
  int paid;
  String user;
}
```

Now you need to add all these DTOs to your schemas library.

**17.** Open `lib/shared/schemas.dart`, and ensure it matches the **Example 10.7** code:

**EXAMPLE 10.7**

```
library ticket_schemas;

import 'package:dartson/dartson.dart';

//Injectables
part 'dtos/base_dto.dart';
part 'dtos/purchase_dto.dart';
part 'dtos/city_dto.dart';
part 'dtos/route_dto.dart';
part 'dtos/time_dto.dart';
part 'dtos/transaction_dto.dart';
```

You should now have a `ticket_schemas` library that is an accurate representation of the seeded data in MongoDB. Each DTO class is marked as a unique @Entity by Dartson and is eligible for JSON serialization and deserialization. Each DTO is a native Dart class, can be passed as a type, has full type checking, and is supported 100 percent by the Dart analyzer and IDEA IDE tooling. It is available to both the web client and the server.

## CREATING A MONGOMODEL WITH CRUD

Now that you have Dart classes that represent your data and an approach to easily serialize JSON to those classes, you are going to build a class that implements basic CRUD actions on the MongoDB instance while using your DTO classes to serialize and deserialize the data.

You'll be implementing the basic Create, Read, Update, and Delete methods along with some helper functionality to handle conversion between different data structures.

Let's create the initial file.

1. From the IDEA project panel, Control-click the `bin` folder, select New > File, and name the file `mongo_model.dart`.

2. Set up `mongo_model.dart` to contain the **Example 10.8** structure:

**EXAMPLE 10.8**

```
library ticket_models;

import 'dart:async';
import 'dart:mirrors';
import 'package:mongo_dart/mongo_dart.dart';

import 'mongo_pool.dart';
import 'package:tickets/shared/schemas.dart';
import 'package:connection_pool/connection_pool.dart';

class MongoModel {

}
```

Let's take a look at what you just did:

- You defined a new library named `ticket_models`.
- In the imports, you included two Dart core libraries and the `mongo_dart` library that you installed into your packages folder via Pub.
- You imported two of your own libraries. You imported the `mongo_pool.dart` file, exposing the `MongoDbPool` class that you declared earlier, and you imported the `schemas.dart` file, exposing the members of the library `ticket_schemas`. Importing the `ticket_schemas` library gives your new class access to all your DTO classes.
- You declared a new class of `MongoModel` that doesn't have any functionality yet.

## INTERFACE METHODS

Before diving into the CRUD actions, let's take a look at a few of the challenges that you will encounter while bringing all these components together. The following code will implement some additional methods used to translate objects into the proper state for their corresponding consumers.

**Challenge:** The `mongo_dart` library is unaware of your DTO structures. In order to enforce a consistent interface across the library, `mongo_dart` uses a class of type `Map` as the preferred data structure. You'll need to convert these `Map` objects to DTOs and vice versa.

**Solution:** You will introduce two functions that use reflection to convert from a DTO class to a Map class. Mirrors and reflection are OK to use when running the DartVM server side.

**Append** the maptoDto and dtoToMap functions to your MongoModel class:

```
dynamic mapToDto(cleanObject, Map document) {
  var reflection = reflect(cleanObject);
  document['id'] = document['_id'].toString();
  document.remove('_id');
  document.forEach((k, v) {
    reflection.setField(new Symbol(k), v);
  });
  return cleanObject;
}


Map dtoToMap(Object object) {
  var reflection = reflect(object);
  Map target = new Map();
  var type = reflection.type;
  while (type != null) {
    type.declarations.values.forEach((item) {
      if (item is VariableMirror) {
        VariableMirror value = item;
        if (!value.isFinal) {
          target[MirrorSystem.getName(value.simpleName)] =
            → reflection.getField(value.simpleName).reflectee;
        }
      }
    });
    type = type.superclass;
    //get properties from superclass too!
  }

  return target;
}
```

**Challenge:** MongoDB represents its unique ID with a field name of _id. Using an underscore as a prefix in Dart enforces library-level privacy. You've told your DTOs to expect an attribute of id to ensure that the value is public.

**Solution:** You will wrap the dtoToMap function in a mongo-specific function that will convert id to _id.

**Append** the dtoToMongoMap function to your MongoModel class:

```
Map dtoToMongoMap(object) {
  Map item = dtoToMap(object);
  // mongo uses an underscore prefix which would act as a private field in dart
  // convert only on write to mongo
  item['_id'] = item['id'];
  item.remove('id');
  return item;
}
```

**Challenge:** You will use the BaseDTO class as the base type for all your method signatures, but there will be cases where you need to instantiate fresh instances of the concrete DTO from only a type and return it to the caller.

**Solution:** You can instantiate an object from a type by using a combination of mirrors and an object's type.

**Append** the getInstance function to your MongoModel class:

```
dynamic getInstance(Type t) {
  MirrorSystem mirrors = currentMirrorSystem();
  LibraryMirror lm = mirrors.libraries.values.firstWhere(
      (LibraryMirror lm) => lm.qualifiedName == new Symbol('ticket_schemas'));
  ClassMirror cm = lm.declarations[new Symbol(t.toString())];
  InstanceMirror im = cm.newInstance(new Symbol(''), []);
  return im.reflectee;
}
```

Your MongoModel class now has all the tools required to expose a CRUD interface using MongoDart and your DTO implementation.

## CONNECT TO MONGO

You will use your MongoDbPool class to manage the connection to the Mongo database. Go ahead and create the instance of MongoDbPool that you'll be using throughout the rest of this chapter by modifying the MongoModel class to include the following:

```
MongoDbPool _dbPool;

MongoModel(String _databaseName, String _databaseUrl, int _databasePoolSize) {
  _dbPool = new MongoDbPool(_databaseUrl + _databaseName, _databasePoolSize);
}
```

The previous code should look somewhat familiar; you're simply passing in your MongoDB credentials. Instead of instantiating Mongo directly, you're using MongoDbPool to handle the number of connections available. You'll be retrieving and returning connections to the pool for each action.

## CREATE

Now, you need to add create functionality to the MongoModel class. Append the **Example 10.9** code to the MongoModel class:

**EXAMPLE 10.9**

```
Future<BaseDTO> createByItem(BaseDTO item) {
    assert(item.id == null);
    item.id = new ObjectId().toString();
    return _dbPool.getConnection().then((ManagedConnection mc) {
        Db db = mc.conn;
        DbCollection collection = db.collection(item.collection_key);
        Map aMap = dtoToMongoMap(item);
        return collection.insert(aMap).then((status) {
            _dbPool.releaseConnection(mc);
            return (status['ok'] == 1) ? item : null;
        });
    });
}
```

Let's take a look at what you did:

- You declared a new asynchronous function that returns a future of type BaseDTO. This ensures that no matter how long the database query takes, your code will wait until the value is ready.

- You checked whether the inbound DTO had an existing ID, and if so you called assert() and forced an error. IDs are assigned only upon creation, so any DTO that already has an ID would mean that it has already been created.

- You asserted that the DTO has no ID, and then assigned the value from ObjectID() to the DTO. ObjectID() is a class exposed by the MongoDart library and will make a Mongo-compliant unique identifier.

- Using the instance of MongoDbPool, you executed an asynchronous call to getConnection() to acquire an open connection to the MongoDB database. The value that is returned is of type ManagedConnection, and the instance has a field named conn. The field conn is an abstract instance of Db from Mongo Dart and is assigned to a typed variable of Db.

**NOTE:** The assignment of the typed variable of Db was done back when you were extending ConnectionPool<T> during the declaration for class MongoDbPool.

- You created a MongoDB-compliant map. Mongo requires that the object written to the database be a map. You also want to match the mongo _id field naming convention. To do so, you created a Map variable and assigned it the response value from the helper method dtoToMongoMap().

- You used the standard MongoDart interface to query a collection. You created a variable reference to the MongoDart collection. You were able to tell MongoDB which collection to select by using the BaseDTO `collection_key` field. You then used the `insert()` method to write your new MongoDB-compliant map to the database.

- After the `insert()` future returned a status value, you returned your database connection to the pool with `releaseConnection()`. Once returned, you moved on to validating the status. The status object is a Map returned after the database executes the query. It contains a field named `status` that tells you if the query was a success. If it was, you always pass back the persisted DTO to the caller—otherwise, you return null.

This method is a great example for all the remaining actions in this chapter. Note that you were able to get all the information you needed from the `BaseDTO` class instance and ignored any of its concrete implementation details.

## DELETE

You need to implement a delete pattern similar to the create action. Append the **Example 10.10** code to your `MongoModel` class:

**EXAMPLE 10.10**

```
Future<Map> deleteByItem(BaseDTO item) async {
  assert(item.id != null);
  return _dbPool.getConnection().then((ManagedConnection mc) {
    Db database = mc.conn;
    DbCollection collection = database.collection(item.collection_key);
    Map aMap = dtoToMongoMap(item);
    return collection.remove(aMap).then((status) {
      _dbPool.releaseConnection(mc);
      return status;
    });
  });
}
```

This implementation should look similar to the code in the "Create" section. Let's take a look at what is different:

- As with the create code, you checked to see if there was an ID. However, when deleting, you want to ensure that it does exist because it needs to have been a previously created object. If it doesn't exist, you run `assert()`.

- The function that is invoked by the collection object is now the `remove()` function.

- The result will always be a status object because this is a destructive action.

## UPDATE

You need to implement an update pattern similar to the create and delete actions. Append the **Example 10.11** code to your MongoModel class:

**EXAMPLE 10.11**

```
Future<Map> updateItem(BaseDTO item) async {
  assert(item.id != null);
  return _dbPool.getConnection().then((ManagedConnection mc) async {
    Db database = mc.conn;
    DbCollection collection = new DbCollection(database, item.collection_key);
    Map selector = {'_id': item.id};
    Map newItem = dtoToMongoMap(item);
    return collection.update(selector, newItem).then((status) {
      _dbPool.releaseConnection(mc);
      return status;
    });
  });
}
```

The implementation should look fairly similar to the code in the "Create" and "Delete" sections.

Let's take a look at what is different:

- You defined a selector object, which is used to query the specific document from the database that matches the DTO ID.
- You invoked the update() function on the collection object. The method accepts two arguments: a query object to find the document in the database, and a document. Note that this approach expects the entire document to be overwritten.

## READ

You need to implement a couple of methods to allow you to read by different criteria. You're going to assume that a read action can result in a collection of documents being returned.

1. Append the **Example 10.12** code to the MongoModel class:

   **EXAMPLE 10.12**

   ```
   Future<List> _getCollection(String collectionName, [Map query = null]) {
     return _dbPool.getConnection().then((ManagedConnection mc) async {
       DbCollection collection = new DbCollection(mc.conn, collectionName);
       return collection.find(query).toList().then((List<Map> maps){
         _dbPool.releaseConnection(mc);
         return maps;
   ```

```
      });
   });
}
```

Let's take a look at what you did:

- You created a generic getter for any given collection. You also accepted a second optional parameter with a Mongo query object.
- You followed the convention established for managing database connections.
- You invoked the `find()` method on the collection object. You used the `await` keyword to mimic a synchronous call. When the query returned, you invoked the method `toList()` to get a list of map items for conversion to DTOs.

2. Append the **Example 10.13** code to the `MongoModel` class:

**EXAMPLE 10.13**

```
Future<List> _getCollectionWhere(String collectionName, fieldName, values) {
  return _dbPool.getConnection().then((ManagedConnection mc) async {
    Db database = mc.conn;
    DbCollection collection = new DbCollection(database, collectionName);
    SelectorBuilder builder = where.oneFrom(fieldName, values);
    return collection.find( builder ).toList().then((map) {
      _dbPool.releaseConnection(mc);
      return map;
    });
  });
}
```

Let's take a look at what you did:

- You created a generic getter for a collection of documents that leverage the `where` operator to filter the response.
- You followed the convention established for managing database connections.
- You created a variable of type `SelectorBuilder` from the Mongo Dart library to construct a query object capable of executing your filter.

Now that you have your helper functions in place, let's implement the various read actions.

3. Append the **Example 10.14** code to the `MongoModel` class:

**EXAMPLE 10.14**

```
//refresh an item from the database instance
Future<BaseDTO> readItemByItem(BaseDTO matcher) async {
  assert(matcher.id != null);
  Map query = {'_id': matcher.id};
```

```
    BaseDTO bDto;
    return _getCollection(matcher.collection_key, query).then((items) {
      bDto = mapToDto(getInstance(matcher.runtimeType), items.first);
      return bDto;
    });
}


//acquires a collection of documents based off a type, and field values
Future<List> readCollectionByTypeWhere(t, fieldName, values) async {
  List list = new List();
  BaseDTO freshInstance = getInstance(t);
  return _getCollectionWhere(freshInstance.collection_key, fieldName,
  → values).then((items) {
    items.forEach((item) {
      list.add(mapToDto(getInstance(t), item));
    });
    return list;
  });
}


//acquires a collection of documents based off a type and an optional query
Future<List> readCollectionByType(t, [Map query = null]) async {
  List list = new List();
  BaseDTO freshInstance = getInstance(t);
  return _getCollection(freshInstance.collection_key, query).then( (items) {
    items.forEach((item) {
      list.add(mapToDto(getInstance(t), item));
    });
    return list;
  });
}
```

These read actions are all variations on patterns we've covered in this chapter. You should now be able to read items from the database based on the current item, a collection of items of the same type, or a collection of items of the same type with matching field values.

## DROP

Although not part of the generic CRUD description, you're also going to add support for dropping a database. This will be useful in later chapters for tearing down databases that are used only for testing. Append the **Example 10.15** code to the MongoModel class:

**EXAMPLE 10.15**

```
Future<Map> dropDatabase() async {
   var connection = await _dbPool.getConnection();
    var database = connection.conn;
    Map status = await database.drop();
    return status;
}
```

# SUMMARY

Congratulations, you have created the data structures and the low-level model that will power your ticketing application. MongoModel is the low-level interface that you can build your business logic on top of. In the next chapter, we'll implement some unit tests to ensure your lasting confidence in your MongoModel class.

## YOU SHOULD NOW KNOW:

- How connection pooling works
- How to implement the connection_pool library
- The challenges of Dart and JSON and their type systems
- How Dartson enables serialization on both client and server
- The impact of reflection on dart2JS-compiled code
- How to include multiple DTOs in a single library
- How to establish a connection to your MongoDB database through ConnectionPool
- Some caveats of working with ObjectIDs in Dart
- The type of objects the MongoDB Dart library expects
- How to write a function to expose document creation for MongoDB
- How to write a function to expose document retrieval for MongoDB
- How to write a function to expose document updates for MongoDB
- How to write a function to expose document deletion for MongoDB

CHAPTER 11

# Webserver and Middleware

In this chapter, you will go through the basics of setting up a web server and exposing a JSON API. Dart ships with a built-in library named HTTPServer for serving content over the Hyper Text Transfer Protocol (HTTP). The HttpServer class acts as the foundation for implementing futures-based request and response handlers.

The HttpServer class is extremely extensible and is used as the foundation for many higher-level server libraries. One of those libraries is named Shelf and is a Google-supported project for composing web servers and other middleware. In Chapter 12, you'll be taking a look at how to use Shelf to build out a RESTful API for your ticketing application.

# SHELF

Shelf provides a consistent pattern for implementing off-the-shelf components for extending a web server. Some of the available components include Shelf Routing, Shelf IO, Shelf Proxy, Shelf Rest, Shelf Auth, and many others. In this chapter, you'll primarily be working with Shelf IO and Shelf Routing.

Shelf enforces a convention that allows developers to declare the correct logic for an inbound *request* and serve up the appropriate *response*. Shelf is composed of a series of handlers and middleware that let a developer control the common execution flow, routing, and object modifications that result from an inbound HTTP request.

# SETTING UP A SHELF EXAMPLE

You're going to install the libraries `shelf`, `shelf_route`, and `shelf_static`. The `shelf` library provides the functionality for composing multiple middleware pieces together. Next, you'll create the basic structure to support what will eventually become your production web server code.

1. From the IDEA project panel, open `pubspec.yaml`, and add the following lines of code to your dependencies:

   ```
   shelf: ">=0.6.2 <0.7.0"
   shelf_static: "0.2.2"
   shelf_route: "0.13.0"
   ```

2. Click Get Dependencies to download the libraries to your packages folder.

   ```
   Got dependencies!
   ```

3. In the IDEA project panel, Control-click the `bin` folder, select New > File, and name the file `webserver.dart`.

   In the following sections, you'll use the `webserver.dart` file to launch a standalone web server using Shelf.

4. Add the **Example 11.1** code to your `webserver.dart` file:

   **EXAMPLE 11.1**

   ```dart
   import 'package:shelf/shelf.dart';
   import 'package:shelf/shelf_io.dart' as io;

   void main() {
     Middleware mw = logRequests();
     Pipeline pl = new Pipeline();
   ```

```
pl = pl.addMiddleware( mw );
Handler handler = pl.addHandler( echo );

io.serve(handler, '0.0.0.0', 8080).then((server) {
  print('Serving at http://${server.address.host}:${server.port}');
});
}


Response echo(Request request) {
  return new Response.ok('Request for "${request.url}"');
}
```

Let's take a look at what you just did inside your main() function:

- Middleware: You acquired an instance of a piece of logging middleware exposed by the shelf library via the logRequest() method. Generally speaking, middleware is a self-contained unit of logic that acts upon a Request to compose a Response.

    This particular middleware component implements a standard approach to outputting log data for every request processed by the Shelf web server. Other examples of middleware could be caching, authentications, header modifications, and so on.

- Pipeline: You instantiated an instance of class Pipeline. Pipeline is a helper class exposed by the shelf library. Its primary function is to act as a queue manager for your middleware processing chain. This means that each middleware component added will place its corresponding logic next in the execution queue. Each piece of middleware will include its own Request parser and Response handler.

- addMiddleware(): You provided your logging middleware to the Pipeline instance as an argument to the addMiddleware() function. The response returns a new Pipeline object with the logging functionality now included. If you had added additional middleware logic that you wanted for your server, you would continue to append it using this method.

- Handler: A handler is a function that is executed in order to process an HTTP request.

    In the case of middleware, handlers wrap other handlers to allow the chain to continue executing in sequential order. In the case of a pipeline, the exposed handler is the *final* method executed. In this example, you simply provide function echo that returns a Response object containing a string of the requested URL.

- Request and Response: Included in the shelf library are two classes: one for Request and one for Response. These classes will instantiate objects that conform to the HTTP object specifications.

- io.serve(): This method is a wrapper for the Dart HttpServer instance. Its method signature requires a handler, server address, and server port. At this point, your handler is composed of one piece of logging middleware and one handler that returns a Response object. For this example, you'll just assign the running server to 0.0.0.0, exposing localhost on a port of 8080.

5. Now that your basic web server is written, you will launch it and test it. In the IDEA editor window, click Run and select "Debug webserver.dart."

6. Launch a web browser of your choice, and navigate to http://localhost:8080.

   In the browser you should see "Request For """.

   In the output window you should see:

   ```
   Serving at http://localhost:8080
   2015-08-10 20:26:19.540  0:00:00.002162  GET  [200]  /
   ```

7. Navigate your browser to http://localhost:8080/dartlang.

   In the browser you should see "Request For 'dartlang'".

   In the output window you should see:

   ```
   Serving at http://localhost:8080
   2015-08-10 20:26:19.540  0:00:00.002162  GET  [200]  /dartlang
   ```

8. Kill the active server process.

## ADDING MIDDLEWARE

Let's modify the previous example to include an additional piece of custom middleware. We want to future-proof the API to enable CORS (cross-origin resource sharing) headers. CORS headers configure access rights between multiple domains. While in the browser, CORS enables sites under domain *alpha.com* to securely load assets from domain *beta.com*, while still preventing *delta.com* from loading the same assets.

When a browser loads an external API for the first time, many browsers send out what is referred to as a preflight test. This test probes the web server to see if there is an associated CORS policy object that defines the access rights.

We want the middleware to intercept any preflight tests and return the expected CORS object in the HTTP response header.

1. Add the **Example 11.2** code after your main() function:

**EXAMPLE 11.2**

```
Map CORSHeader = {'content-type': 'text/json',
  'Access-Control-Allow-Origin': '*',
  'Access-Control-Allow-Headers': "Origin, X-Requested-With,
  → Content-Type, Accept",
```

```
    'Access-Control-Allow-Methods': "POST, GET, PUT, DELETE, OPTIONS"};

Middleware corsMiddleWare = createMiddleware(requestHandler: reqHandler,
 → responseHandler: respHandler);

Response reqHandler(Request request){
  if(request.method == "OPTIONS")
  {
    return new Response.ok(null, headers: CORSHeader);
  }
  return null; // nothing to see here... move along
}


Response respHandler(Response response) {
  return response.change(headers: CORSHeader);
}
```

Let's take a look at what you just did:

- createMiddleware: The `shelf` library exposes a method named `createMiddleware()` that is a pseudo-factory that creates a middleware instance. The method accepts two named parameters as arguments, one for the `Request` parsing and one for the `Response` handling. You passed in two custom functions that contain the business logic for your CORS policy.

- CORSHeader: You created a `Map` `CORSHeader` using the Map literal syntax and a series of key–value string pairs. At a high level, you set the expectation that you will be returning JSON, you will accept the default HTTP methods with the addition of `OPTIONS`, and you will allow a request that originates from any domain.

> **NOTE:** Diving into a full breakdown of a CORS object is outside the scope of this book. For more information, please see https://developer.mozilla.org/en-US/docs/Web/HTTP/Access_control_CORS.

- reqHandler: The Request handler is the focal point for this piece of middleware. All inbound requests inspect the HTTP method. If the `OPTIONS` method is detected, you handle it as a preflight request and send back an immediate `Response` with the CORS object appended to the headers. Sending back `null` in any `Request` `Middleware` handler will allow the next handler in the chain to inspect the request.

- resHandler: The Response handler is called on the other end of the chain. Once the last Request handler is called, all other response handlers in the chain are executed in a FILO order. In the case of the CORS response handler, you want to ensure that all HTTP responses have the proper CORS object in the HTTP header. You leveraged the `response.change()` method to append your existing CORS objects on the message header.

Now that you have the logic to create the `Middleware` instance, in the next step you'll modify your pipeline to include the CORS logic.

2. Modify the code in your `main()` function to reflect the code in **Example 11.3**:

**EXAMPLE 11.3**

```
void main() {
  Middleware mw = logRequests();
  Pipeline pl = new Pipeline();
  pl = pl.addMiddleware( corsMiddleWare ).addMiddleware( mw );
  Handler handler = pl.addHandler( echo );

  io.serve(handler, '0.0.0.0', 8080).then((server) {
    print('Serving at http://${server.address.host}:${server.port}');
  });
}
```

Now let's run the server and inspect the HTTP responses that are generated.

3. In the IDEA top bar, click Run and then select "Debug webserver.dart."

Next, you're going to mimic an `OPTIONS` call using a command-line tool named CURL.

4. Open your system terminal, and execute the following CURL command:

```
$ curl -i -X OPTIONS http://localhost:8080/
```

5. Inspect the response from the previous command to ensure the CORS object is in the header.

```
HTTP/1.1 200 OK
access-control-allow-headers: Origin, X-Requested-With, Content-Type, Accept
access-control-allow-origin: *
access-control-allow-methods: POST, GET, PUT, DELETE, OPTIONS
x-frame-options: SAMEORIGIN
content-type: text/json
server: dart:io with Shelf
```

6. Kill the active server process.

# ADDING ROUTING

Routing is the logic that interprets what code should handle and support business logic for an inbound HTTP request base on its URI. In an MVC framework, routes usually point to a controller that will instantiate dependencies and wire up data. You'll be hooking up the routes to controllers in the next chapter, but for now let's just take a look at how to implement different types of routes and declare some simple handlers.

To discern the intent of a request, frameworks leverage the HTTP method attributes found on an inbound request object. HTTP specifies method attribute values. The values of interest to most routing logic are POST, GET, PUT, and DELETE. In our case, these methods will pair with the following actions from the CRUD actions:

- POST maps to Create.
- GET maps to Read.
- PUT maps to Update.
- DELETE maps to Delete.

In the previous example, you had a single global handler for any request that hit the server. That doesn't scale when implementing business logic. Let's declare some new route handlers routed by their HTTP methods and URI structure. To do so you'll be creating a router object.

Change your `webserver.dart` to reflect the changes in **Example 11.4**:

**EXAMPLE 11.4**

```dart
import 'package:shelf/shelf.dart';
import 'package:shelf/shelf_io.dart' as io;
import 'package:shelf_route/shelf_route.dart';

void main() {

  Router primaryRouter = router();
  Router api = primaryRouter.child('/api');

  api.post('/user', (Request request) async {
    return new Response.ok('Success!' + await request.readAsString() );
  });

  api.get('/user/{name}/{id}', (Request request) {
    var id = getPathParameter(request, 'id');
```

```
      var name = getPathParameter(request, 'name');
      return new Response.ok('Success! Found: ' + id + ' ' + name );
    });

    Middleware mw = logRequests();
    Pipeline pl = new Pipeline();
    pl = pl.addMiddleware( corsMiddleWare ).addMiddleware( mw );
    Handler apiHandler = pl.addHandler( primaryRouter.handler );

    io.serve(apiHandler, '0.0.0.0', 8080).then((server) {
      print('Serving at http://${server.address.host}:${server.port}');
    });
}
```

Let's take a look at what you just did inside the `main()` function:

- Router: You instantiated a router object. This will contain the primary route branching logic for inbound HTTP requests.

- `child`: To write terse code and avoid typos, `Router` supports the concept of nested routes. By invoking the `child()` method, any route appended to the returned router will be prefixed with the string URI segment `'/api'`.

- `post`: You declared your first route by invoking the `post()` method on the `api` object. You pass the URI segment of `'user'` and then register the request handler. The handler itself is an asynchronous function that returns a response object.

  By invoking `ok()` on the response object, you set it to a status code of 200 with a body of the provided string argument.

- `get`: You declared your second route in a similar fashion to the first. The first difference being that this route resolves to HTTP requests that provide a GET method.

  The Shelf library itself exposes a method of `getPathParameter()`, which can retrieve the parameters that are defined in the route and which are then sent on the raw request object. In this case you're retrieving the {name} and {id} parameters. You can mix and match these approaches to handle a majority of the use cases a RESTful API will require.

- Handler: You ended by adding the `Router` handler to the pipeline, bypassing it as an argument to the `addHandler()` method of `Pipeline`. By making the router the final handler, you are ensuring that all middleware `Request` actions occur prior to the business logic, and that all middleware `Response` actions occur after our business logic. This is a key distinction between middleware and a router. Middleware occurs on all HTTP occurrences, whereas a router handler gets activated only if there is a matching URI pattern.

# SERVING STATIC ASSETS

So far we've looked at how to write a web response for managing a data API. Now you need to configure your web server to work with static assets. This use case will be useful when you deploy your application to an externally hosted provider. For now, you can test serving assets after they've been compiled using Pub build and dart2js.

Shelf has a prebuilt handler named `shelf_static` that is a public library and facilitates reading files from the file system and returning the file to the caller. You'll also be leveraging some of the built-in Dart libraries to get the current directory information and platform details.

1. Add the following imports to your `webserver.dart` file:

```
import 'dart:io';
import 'dart:async';
import 'package:path/path.dart';
import 'package:shelf_static/shelf_static.dart';
```

In the following code, the library `shelf_static` will expose a method named `createStaticHandler()`. When completed, the handler will match the URI fragments to find files on the file system. To configure the handler, the method needs the path to the directory in which your assets are stored and a default file.

According to the Dart directory structure guide, all your published assets should be exported to a folder named `build/web`. That location is the destination folder for the Pub build process. Even with that, the web server still needs the full directory path on your file system. The Dart VM exposes the data about the current running location and surfaces it via the platform library.

2. Append the **Example 11.5** to the top of your `main()` function:

**EXAMPLE 11.5**

```
void main() {
  var path = Platform.script.toFilePath();
  var currentDirectory = dirname(path);
  var fullPath = join(currentDirectory, '..', 'build/web');
  Handler fHandler = createStaticHandler(fullPath, defaultDocument:
  → 'index.html');
  ...
  ...
}
```

Let's take a look at what you just did:

- path: You used the `Platform` class exposed by the `dart:io` library to expose the full path of the currently executing Dart script. This works locally or when you deploy to production.

- currentDirectory: You used a `dirname()` method exposed by the `path` library to strip the provided path down to its directory by removing the script name.

- fullPath: You used the `join()` method exposed by the `path` library to assemble each argument into a string value with the correct corresponding slashes and trailing slashes.

- fHandler: You assigned an instance of a handler from the pseudo-factory `createStaticHandler()` method. This is just like any other Shelf `Handler` class object and could be immediately placed onto the pipeline.

You now have a handler that can read your local file system and return HTML, CSS, images, and many other types of assets. Next we'll take a look at how to fork the handling of both data and assets.

## USING MULTIPLE HANDLERS

If you remember the discussion on the pipeline object, I talked about a pipeline being a chain of request and response handlers, all of which end with a final pipeline handler. You are now faced with a dilemma where you have constructed an API handler and a handler that specializes in serving static assets. You're going to bring these together using a class named Cascade.

A cascade is a way to group multiple pipelines together by declaring them hierarchically. You can add a pipeline to the cascade queue by passing the pipeline's handler object as an argument to Cascade's add() method.

A cascade will be executed as a FIFO queue. Any response that results in a status code of 200 will terminate the cascade and return the response to the caller. All remaining handlers will be skipped. All of this culminates in the cascade object exposing a single handler instance that can be passed into our server.

Go ahead and modify your main() function to implement a cascade:

```
Cascade cc = new Cascade().add(apiHandler).add(fHandler);
io.serve(cc.handler, '0.0.0.0', 8080).then((server) {
  print('Serving at http://${server.address.host}:${server.port}');
});
```

## SETTING UP AND BUILDING YOUR WEB FOLDER

To serve up web assets, you will need a web folder and associated HTML files. For the purposes of this task, you will keep the structure simple. You'll be looking at how to structure your web assets in detail in later chapters.

1. In the IDEA project panel, Control-click the `tickets` folder, select New > Directory, and name the directory `web`.

2. Control-click the web folder, select New > File, and name the file `index.html`.

3. Add the **Example 11.6** HTML to the index.html file:

**EXAMPLE 11.6**

```
<!DOCTYPE html>
<html lang="en">
<head>
    <meta charset="utf-8">
    <title>Ticket Application</title>
</head>
<body>
    <p>Dart Ticket Application<p>
</body>
</html>
```

4. Open Terminal and execute the following command inside the root directory of your tickets project:

```
$ pub build
Loading source assets...
Loading dartson transformers...
Building tickets...
Built 2 files to "build".
```

Let's take a look at what you just did:

- The Pub package layout convention describes the dependencies that the Pub tool expects a project to have. You are adhering to their web asset folder naming convention to leverage pub build.

- You generated a bare-bones HTML index file that can be used to serve up when a request is made that does not match the Data API URI conventions.

- You executed the pub build command in the Terminal. This tells Pub that you want to generate a build that can be used for production. If you had Dart code in the web folder, it would be transpiled out to JavaScript. In this case, you're just copying over your index.html file into the build/web folder so that your static asset server will have a file to read.

## CALLING STATIC ASSETS AND QUERYING THE API

You now have all the components you need in place to run an API and asset server from the same Dart server instance. Let's go ahead and ensure it works as expected. Since we have yet to implement any visual aspects of the page, we can use the command-line tool `curl` to ensure that we get proper HTTP responses from the web server.

1. From the command line, change into your project directory, run `webserver.dart`, and then execute the following commands:

```
$ dart bin/webserver.dart &
$ curl -H "Content-Type: application/json" -X POST -d '{"username":"xyz",
→ "password":"xyz"}' http://localhost:8080/api/user
Success!{"username":"xyz","password":"xyz"}%
$ curl http://localhost:8080/api/user/carl/13
Success! Found: 13 carl%
$ curl http://localhost:8080/index.html
<!DOCTYPE html>
<html lang="en">
<head>
    <meta charset="utf-8">
    <title>Ticket Application</title>
</head>
<body>
<p>Dart Ticket Application<p>
</body>
</html>
```

2. Kill your Dart web server using the following command:

```
$ pkill -f dart
[1]  + 4286 terminated  dart bin/webserver.dart
```

# SUMMARY

Congratulations, you've run through the basics of setting up a deployable web server. Throughout the rest of this book, you'll be building on this example, so make sure that it's working well and that you understand the core concepts. One thing to be aware of is that you have this configured to serve up only assets from the build folder, so making changes to the HTML or assets will not be reflected until you run pub build again. Because of that, and because we like testing our code using the DartVM inside Chromium, you'll continue to use the built-in Pub Serve functionality when testing locally. However, when you get to the chapters about deploying to production, your server code will be ready to go.

## YOU SHOULD NOW KNOW:

- What the Shelf framework solves compared to the HttpServer library
- What a handler is
- What the theory of middleware is, and what Shelf's Middleware class is
- What a route is
- What a cascade is
- What a request is
- What a response is
- What a CORS policy is
- How to acquire URL parameters from a route

# CHAPTER 12

# API Routing, Requests, and Responses

In the previous chapter, you explored the basic principles needed to manage and maintain a robust HTTP server using Shelf. In this chapter, you'll be leveraging your Shelf implementation to expose a RESTful API that your ticket application can use.

Before you get to serving up responses, you need to implement the business logic that powers your ticket application. You'll be implementing a simplified model–view–controller (MVC) pattern for which you'll write some generic helper functionality to facilitate communication between your routing logic, your model, and your controllers.

# MODELING YOUR TICKETING DOMAIN

Back in Chapter 10, you built a class named MongoModel that implemented basic CRUD functionality for your database. It used a series of DTO objects to act as a schema enforcer for the data structures inside your MongoDB database. You will now leverage that functionality to allow a new class, named TicketingModel, to interact with the database, encapsulate your business logic, and return responses containing your application data.

From the IDEA project panel, Control-click the bin folder, select New > File, and name the file ticketing_model.dart. Then enter the **Example 12.1** code in your new file:

**EXAMPLE 12.1**

```
import 'dart:async';
import 'mongo_model.dart';
import 'package:tickets/shared/schemas.dart';
import 'package:tickets/db/db_config.dart';
import 'package:dartson/dartson.dart';

class TicketingModel {
  MongoModel _mongo;

  TicketingModel() {
    DbConfigValues config = new DbConfigValues();
    _mongo = new MongoModel(config.dbName, config.dbURI, config.dbSize);
  }
}
```

This pattern should look familiar. Let's take a look at what you just did:

- import: You imported your library dependencies. The imports here should all be familiar to you from earlier chapters. At a high level, they provide database and DTO functionality.
- TicketingModel: You implemented a new class named TicketingModel. This is the class you'll use to encapsulate your business logic.
- MongoModel: You instantiated an instance of MongoModel to enable database interactions. You'll retrieve your DTOs from this instance throughout the rest of this chapter.

## USING A CONSISTENT METHOD SIGNATURE

Now that your class is ready, take a moment to think about the requirements for what a consistent method signature would look like. Your logic is likely to have two consistent features: It needs to support asynchronous calls, and it will likely take in a multitude of parameters formats.

The REST specifications allow for URL parameters, query parameters, and JSON in the post body. With that in mind, you need to standardize on each method accepting a map as an argument and a future as a response type. The rest of the methods in your class will resemble the following pattern:

```
Future methodName(Map params) {
  return _mongo.action(DTO);
}
```

By following this format, you'll be able to write generic parsing functionality throughout the chapter.

## GETTING COLLECTIONS OF DATA

Look over your wireframes from Chapter 7 to determine how best to begin getting the data. Start by exposing two end points, the first of which should return the full list of destination cities and the second of which should return all available flight times. This functionality is supported natively from your MongoModel class and results in no additional parsing logic.

Add the methods in **Example 12.2** to your TicketingModel class:

**EXAMPLE 12.2**
```
Future getAllCities(Map params) {
  return _mongo.readCollectionByType(CityDTO);
}

Future getAllTimes(Map params) {
  return _mongo.readCollectionByType(TimeDTO);
}
```

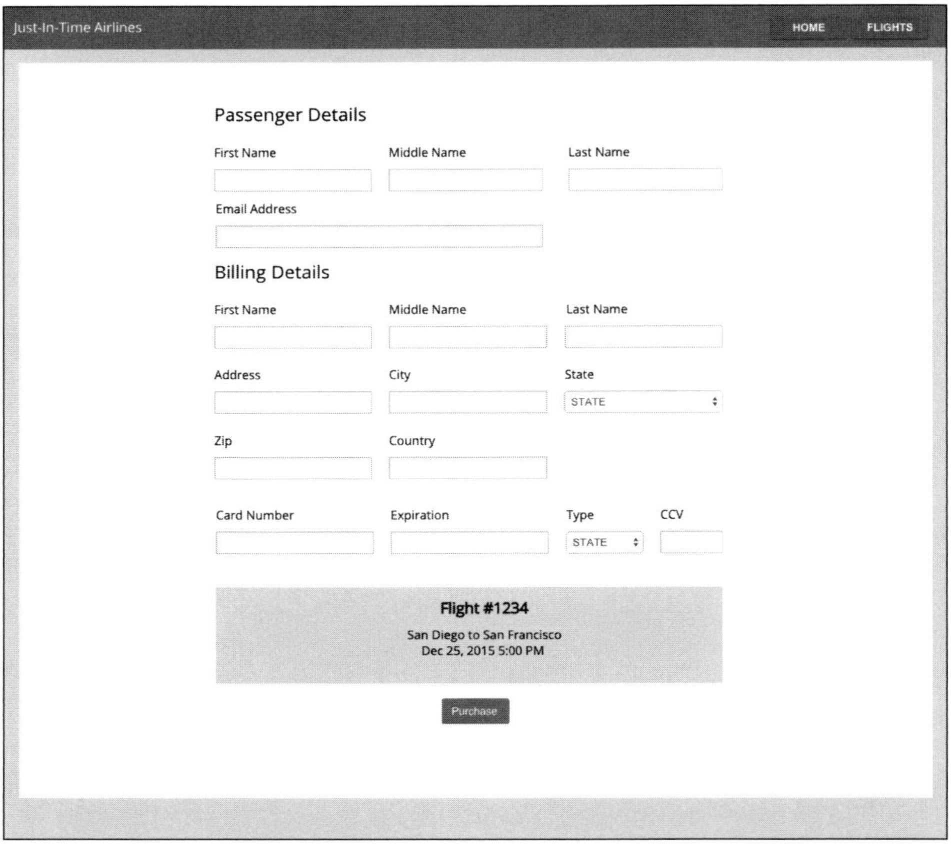

FIGURE 12.1
Order form

**Flight #1234**

San Diego to San Francisco
Dec 25, 2015 5:00 PM

## CREATING MULTIPLE ASYNCHRONOUS WRITES

Review the order form from Chapter 7, shown here in **Figure 12.1**. It not only has a call to record a ticket order, but it also has a step where you would have to make a call to a third-party credit card processor. Implementing a payment gateway is outside the scope of this book, but you will at least mimic recording a transaction to the database.

Another concern is code re-use. Forms are historically regression prone because they can contain a very long list of object attributes that you need to keep in sync between the client and server. Luckily, you used a DTO approach to share code between the client and server. You will use the PurchaseDTO class to shuttle data between both tiers.

Add the method in **Example 12.3** to your TicketingModel class:

**EXAMPLE 12.3**

```
Future createPurchase(Map params) async {
  var dson = new Dartson.JSON();
  PurchaseDTO purchaseDTO = dson.map(params, new PurchaseDTO() );

  TransactionDTO tDTO = new TransactionDTO();
  tDTO.paid = 1000;  //we're faking a successful creditcard payment
  tDTO.user = purchaseDTO.pEmail;

  await _mongo.createByItem(tDTO); //nested async call
  purchaseDTO.transactionId = tDTO.id;
  return _mongo.createByItem(purchaseDTO);
}
```

Let's take a look at what you just did:

- Map: You followed the convention outlined earlier, and you expect a map as a parameter.
- Dartson: You instantiated an instance of Dartson using the JSON factory constructor. This sets the encoding type for all further actions to default to JSON. The dson.map() function takes two arguments: The first is your map post object, and the second is a new instance of the purchaseDTO variable. The dson.map() function will use reflection to assign the values from the map post object to the corresponding attributes on the PurchaseDTO instance.
- PurchaseDTO: You assigned the purchaseDTO to the response instance from dson.map(). It now contains all the posted values as a native Dart class, and it can also be persisted to your Mongo database.
- TransactionDTO: You created a new instance of a TransactionDTO named tDTO. This will be used to track the amount paid by a user, so you acquire their email address from the PurchaseDTO. This fakes the recording of a credit card transaction.
- createItemByItem: You leveraged the functionality of MongoModel to first write out TransactionDTO to the database. By using the await keyword, you mimicked synchronous behavior. Finally, you used the returned instance of the TransactionDTO to acquire a MongoDB ObjectID and assigned it as the transaction value of the PurchaseDTO.

  This will allow you to look up transaction records in a user's purchase history. You then wrote the contents of the PurchaseDTO instance to the database while maintaining the same instance for further use.

The createPurchase() method has a lot of overlapping concepts in it. It's exciting to see so many of your components working together to create concise and powerful code.

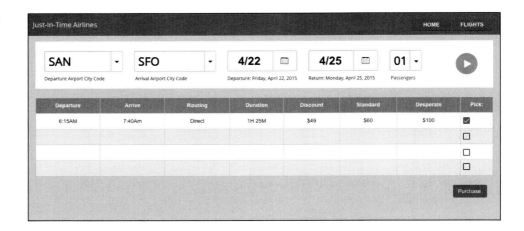

**FIGURE 12.2** Flights

## NESTING DTOS

To render the flight display from Chapter 7, shown here in **Figure 9.2**, you will create a nested DTO. This means a DTO with another DTO as a field. Your response includes a list of TimeDTOs, where each TimeDTO contains a corresponding RouteDTO. This requires two calls to the MongoDB database.

In the previous code for createPurchase(), the object posted to the API corresponded to a DTO you created back in Chapter 7. Let's take a look at an example where you use parameters from a post object to return a valid DTO from MongoDB.

1. Append the **Example 12.4** code to your TicketModel class:

**EXAMPLE 12.4**

```
Future getTimesByCity(Map params) async {
  Map queryTime = {'arrival': params['cityArrival'],
                   'departure': params['cityDepart']};

  List<TimeDTO> time_dtos;
  time_dtos = await _mongo.readCollectionByType(TimeDTO, queryTime);

  Map queryRoutes = {'route':params['cityDepart']+ "_"
+params['cityArrival'] };
  return _mongo.readCollectionByType(RouteDTO, queryRoutes)
   → .then((List rdtos) {
    time_dtos.forEach((TimeDTO dto) => dto.route = rdtos.first);
```

```
    return time_dtos;
  });
}
```

Let's take a look at what you just did:

- Map: You followed the convention outlined earlier, and you expect a map to be supplied as a parameter.
- queryTime and queryRoutes: You created query objects that you can pass to MongoModel. In this case, you used the key–value pairs that are part of the map post parameter.
- TimeDTO: You used the query object in conjunction with the readCollectionByType() function. This returns a list of the associated TimeDTOs.
- RouteDTO: The route data has a unique ID composed of both cities involved. You concatenated the two city strings and created a new query to acquire the corresponding route information. You then assigned the first RouteDTO response as the value for the route field on TimeDTO.

Notice in Figure 12.2 that you have similar requirements to show flight recap information. Depending on the context in which the page is instantiated, you might have only the flight number available. You need to show time and route information. You need to expose an API to retrieve TimeDTOs from only a flight number.

2. Append the **Example 12.5** code to your TicketModel class:

**EXAMPLE 12.5**

```
Future getTimesByFlightNumber(Map params) async {
  List<TimeDTO> time_dtos;
  time_dtos = await _mongo.readCollectionByType(TimeDTO,
  → {'flight': int.parse(params['flight'])} );
  var query = {'route': time_dtos.first.departure + "_" +
  → time_dtos.first.arrival};
  return _mongo.readCollectionByType(RouteDTO, query).then((List rdtos) {
    time_dtos.forEach((TimeDTO dto) => dto.route = rdtos.first);
    return time_dtos;
  });
}
```

The logic here should look very similar to the getTimesByCity() method. The only difference is that your TimeDTOs are queried using a flight ID integer. With that, you have wrapped up the foundations for the API queries that you will be using for the rest of the book.

# IMPLEMENTING CONTROLLERS

Let's prepare your project to contain controller code:

1. From the IDEA project panel, open pubspec.yaml, and add the following line to your dependencies:

   shelf_path: "0.1.5"

2. Click Get Dependencies to download the libraries to your packages folder.

   Got dependencies!

3. From the IDEA project panel, Control-click the bin folder, select New > File, and name the file ticketing_controller.dart.

   Your project should now be ready to add controller code.

4. Append the **Example 12.6** code to your ticketing_controller.dart file:

   **EXAMPLE 12.6**

   ```
   library ticket_controller;

   import 'package:shelf/shelf.dart';
   import 'package:shelf_path/shelf_path.dart' as path;
   import 'ticketing_model.dart';
   import 'dart:async';
   import 'dart:convert';
   import 'package:dartson/dartson.dart';

   TicketingModel model = new TicketingModel();
   Dartson converter = new Dartson.JSON();
   ```

In a classic MVC pattern, the controller's job is to act as the glue between the view and the model. Ideally, controllers are kept extremely thin and allow views to be decoupled from their model implementations.

You will implement a generic controller that will handle serving data to your Shelf requests. In the "Modeling Your Ticket Domain" section of this chapter, you implemented a consistent method signature across all your functions. That signature simply expects a map object that contains all the posted fields.

Although this approach simplifies what is expected, it means you have to boil down all your possible HTTP payload structures to a unified format. You're going to add parsing support for two of the most common formats: post parameters and path parameters. The goal is to map all the key–value pairs onto a single payload map object.

## PATH PARAMETERS

Path parameters are derived from the structure of a URI. A URI can contain multiple types of path parameters, including segmented parameters and query parameters.

```
GET /user/123456/comments?stars=5
```

In this example, `/123456/` represents a segmented parameter, whereas `?stars=5` represents a query parameter. Shelf path supports a generic way to acquire both of these. Let's add the **Example 12.7** code to the `ticketing_controller.dart` file:

**EXAMPLE 12.7**

```
Map getPathParams(Request request, Map payload) {
  Map params = path.getPathParameters(request);
  params.forEach( (key, val) {
    payload[key] = val;
  });
  return payload;
}
```

Let's take a look at what you just did:

- `getPathParameters`: You assigned `shelf_path` library to a named identifier of `path`. You leveraged its top-level function to parse your Shelf request object. The response is a generic map with field–value pairs reflecting your named parameters. The request object will contain the actual variable names for your segmented parameters, as defined by Shelf routes. We'll look at Shelf routes shortly.

- `forEach`: You iterated over the parsed objects attributes and assigned the corresponding pairs to your payload object. This payload will be the map that is then supplied as an argument to your `TicketingModel` methods, with all the parameters accessible as map fields.

## POST PARAMETERS

Post parameters are specifically sent using the HTTP method of POST. The REST specification says to expect the actual payload object in the HTTP request body, and the format will be specified by the content-type attribute. In this case, you expect the content type to be JSON. Let's take a look at how to parse a Shelf request. Add the **Example 12.8** code to your controller:

**EXAMPLE 12.8**

```
Future<Map> getPostParams(Request request) {
  return request.readAsString().then( (String body) {
    return body.isNotEmpty ? JSON.decode(body) : {};
  });
}
```

Let's take a look at what you just did:

- readAsString: You used one of the many parsing methods available on the request object. Because you are expecting a JSON string, you called the readAsString() future. This returns the request message body value as a string.

- isNotEmpty: Because you are creating a generic handler that will check both path parameters and post body objects, you want to ensure you always pass at least an empty object forward. If no object exists, you simple pass an empty map literal.

## RESPONSE OBJECTS

So far we've been looking at the client-to-server flow. Let's take a look at what the return trip looks like. For every inbound request, the Shelf library expects a response. In your setup, you need two functions to properly format the outbound response: _dartsonListToJson() and makeResponse(). Let's take a look at the Dartson method first.

1. Append the **Example 12.9** code to your controller:

   **EXAMPLE 12.9**

   ```
   String _dartsonListToJson(payload) {
     var encodable = converter.serialize (payload);
     return JSON.encode(encodable);
   }
   ```

   Let's take a look at what you just did:

   - converter.serialize: The serialize() method is part of the Dartson library. It takes a Dartson-registered entity and converts it into a serializable map.

   - JSON.encode: Once the Dartson entity is converted to a serializable map, common libraries such as JSON can act upon it. This allows you to prepare the modified object to be sent across the wire as a JSON-encoded string.

2. Append the **Example 12.10** code to your library:

   **EXAMPLE 12.10**

   ```
   Future<Response> makeResponse( String json ) async {
     var response = new Response.ok( json );
     return response;
   }
   ```

Let's take a look at what you just did:

- Response.ok: You created a new Response instance. The Response class exposes a series of factory constructors, including ok(), forbidden(), found(), internalServerError(), and other HTTP response statuses. By invoking the ok() method, you set the HTTP response code to 200 and supplied a JSON string as an argument from the previous method.

- Response: You used Dart's built-in async method to convert the returned value to a future and return the new Response with your payload.

## GENERIC JSON HANDLER

Now that you have your request and response parsing parameters in place, let's see what this is going to look like when you put it together.

1. Append the **Example 12.11** code to your controller:

**EXAMPLE 12.11**

```
Future <Response> handleCities(Request request) {
  return _genericJsonHandler(model.getAllCities, request);
}
```

You declared a handler specific to your model.getAllCities call from earlier in the chapter. You passed it as a function reference along with the inbound request.

2. Append the **Example 12.12** code to your library:

**EXAMPLE 12.12**

```
Future <Response> _genericJsonHandler(Function getter, Request request) {
  return getPostParams(request)
  .then( ( params ) => getPathParams( request , params ) )
  .then( ( payload ) => getter( payload ) )
  .then( ( list ) => _dartsonListToJson( list ) )
  .then( makeResponse );
}
```

This code uses future chaining to ensure the proper order of operations. Let's take a look at what you just did:

- getter: You allowed an abstract getter function to be passed in. In this example, it will evaluate to the model.getAllCities reference from earlier. It will represent the function that invoked on the model to return the DTOs from Mongo.

- Request: You parsed your request using two helper methods: getPostParams() and getPathParams().

- payload: After going through both Path and Post parsing functions, you passed your normalized map payload to your getter function. This results in a call to your TicketingModel instance and will yield a valid result from the database.
- dartsonListToJson: Once you had a valid response object, you converted it from the Dartson structure back to JSON.
- makeResponse: Once you had your Dartson object converted back to a string, you instantiated a response object and sent it back to the caller.

## WIRE UP THE REMAINING APIS

Now that you have your generic handler in place, you can quickly wire up different handlers to different models. Append the **Example 12.13** code to your controller:

**EXAMPLE 12.13**

```
Future <Response> handleTimesCity(Request request) {
  return _genericJsonHandler(model.getTimesByCity, request);
}

Future <Response> handleFlightNumber(Request request) {
  return _genericJsonHandler(model.getTimesByFlightNumber, request);
}

Future <Response> handleTimes(Request request) {
  return _genericJsonHandler(model.getAllTimes, request);
}

Future <Response> handlePurchase(Request request) {
  return _genericJsonHandler(model.createPurchase, request);
}
```

This pattern is the union of the model work you did earlier in the chapter, but it now leverages the new generic approach to request and response handling. You just exposed unique handlers for each API route that you're about to wire up.

# HANDLING ROUTES

In Chapter 11 you looked at the power of the Shelf route. At this point you just need to wire up some new end points to your new handlers. Open your `webserver.dart` file, and modify the `main()` function to match **Example 12.14**:

**EXAMPLE 12.14**

```dart
import 'ticketing_controller.dart' as controller;
void main() {

  var path = Platform.script.toFilePath();
  var currentDirectory = dirname(path);
  var fullPath   = join(currentDirectory, '..', 'build/web');
  Handler fHandler  = createStaticHandler(fullPath ,
  → defaultDocument: 'index.html');

  Router primaryRouter = router();
  Router api = primaryRouter.child('/tickets');
  api.add('/flight/{flight}', ['GET'], controller.handleFlightNumber);
  api.add('/cities', ['GET'], controller.handleCities);
  api.add('/times', ['POST'], controller.handleTimesCity);
  api.add('/purchase', ['POST'], controller.handlePurchase);
  Middleware mw = logRequests();
  Pipeline pl = new Pipeline();
  pl = pl.addMiddleware(corsMiddleWare).addMiddleware(mw);
  Handler apiHandler  = pl.addHandler(primaryRouter.handler);

  Cascade cc = new Cascade().add(apiHandler).add(fHandler);

  io.serve(cc.handler, '0.0.0.0',  8080)
      .then( (HttpServer server) => print( 'http serving on: '
      + server.port.toString() ));
}
```

In this code, you've wired up your API to expose end points that correspond to the model functionality from the beginning of the chapter. Each route will result in the generation of a request object that will be sent into its matching controller. Your `TicketingModel` and controller will parse the request, fetch the data from Mongo, and generate a response containing your DTOs.

## TESTING ROUTES

A great way to ensure that your routes are working as expected is to test them using `curl`. Let's take a look at a couple of examples.

Restart your server, and try some of the following commands:

```
$ curl http://localhost:8080/tickets/flight/1016
[{"collection_key":"Times","flight":1016,"departure":"SFO","arrival":
→ "SAN","takeoff":1000,"route":{"collection_key":"Routes","route":
→ "SFO_SAN","duration":145,"price1":49,"price2":79,"price3":99,"seats":7}}]%
```

```
$ curl http://localhost:8080/tickets/cities
[{"collection_key":"Cities","city":"Los Angeles","airportcode":"LAX","gate":
→ "C32"},{"collection_key":"Cities","city":"San Diego","airportcode":
→ "SAN","gate":"B21"},{"collection_key":"Cities","city":"San Francisco",
→ "airportcode":"SFO","gate":"A12"},{"collection_key":"Cities","city":
→ "Oakland","airportcode":"OAK","gate":"B5"},{"collection_key":"Cities",
→ "city":"Sacramento","airportcode":"SMF","gate":"A33"}]%
```

```
$ curl -H "Content-Type: application/json" -X POST -d '{"cityDepart":"SFO",
→ "cityArrival":"SAN","dateDepart":"2015-12-31","dateArrival":"2015-12-31"}'
→ http://localhost:8080/tickets/times/
[{"collection_key":"Times","flight":1016,"departure":"SFO","arrival":"SAN",
→ "takeoff":1000,"route":{"collection_key":"Routes","route":"SFO_SAN",
→ "duration":145,"price1":49,"price2":79,"price3":99,"seats":7}},
→ {"collection_key":"Times","flight":1021,"departure":"SFO","arrival":
→ "SAN","takeoff":1230,"route":{"collection_key":"Routes","route":"SFO_SAN",
→ "duration":145,"price1":49,"price2":79,"price3":99,"seats":7}}]%
```

# SUMMARY

Congratulations, you've just finished building your first fully functional Dart API. You've finally assembled enough of the necessary pieces to do some hefty back-end development using Dart.

This API will power all the front-end Dart development you'll be doing in the next few chapters, so it's important that your code be working. To ensure we have a quality API, you will be taking a look at how to test your code in Chapter 13.

## YOU SHOULD NOW KNOW:

- How to instantiate an instance of `MongoModel`
- How to acquire data from `MongoModel`
- How to parse query parameters
- How to parse segmented parameters
- What the high-level role of a model is
- What the high-level role of a controller is
- How to declare a route handler
- How to create a response object

CHAPTER 13

# Unit Testing
# Your Code

In Chapter 10, you built out the basic functionality for interacting with your Mongo database. You implemented a basic CRUD interface and wrote a handful of helper functions. Your `MongoModel` class now has multiple ways to modify the database based on which type of data transfer object you are working with.

To maintain confidence that the code in your `MongoModel` class is working correctly, you need to write unit tests to ensure that when changes are made, no regressions are introduced.

# WHAT IS UNIT TESTING?

*Unit testing* is a best practice for creating maintainable software. In short, it's a set of functions that represent different scenarios to test the results of other code.

Unit testing frameworks provide helper functions for writing tests and reporting results. Often, unit testing frameworks are designed to run externally from your primary application, and they can often be run as part of your build process.

Because you write and run unit tests outside your primary application, the tests verify the expected results of the code and, by going through the process of using the tested code in a separate context, you are encouraged to write concise, loosely coupled code. Code bases that display these features often end up being more maintainable.

Many different philosophies are associated with unit testing. Two of the more popular philosophies are *test-driven development* and *behavior-driven development*. Many of these philosophies are quite expansive and end up dictating your entire approach to software engineering.

In the context of this book, unit testing is about testing code in small, self-contained chunks. You will learn the basics of writing unit tests and be able to apply your own philosophy as you see fit. Although it's definitely not recommended, your philosophy can even include not writing unit tests; they are completely optional.

# JASMINE VIA GUINNESS

You have many options when choosing a unit testing framework. One of the more popular choices is the Jasmine test framework. Jasmine was originally developed for use in the JavaScript language by developers at Pivotal Labs. It was designed to meet the needs of developers attempting to implement behavior-driven development best practices on the web. The result was an easy-to-use testing framework that, when executed, resulted in human-readable sentences that describe the function being tested. Since its arrival in late 2010, it has been ported to numerous languages and many different development frameworks. Dart's port of Jasmine is titled Guinness and is primarily a community-supported project. Although Guinness is not officially backed by Google, its primary author is a member of the Google Angular team, and the library pairs nicely with Angular Dart.

# SETTING UP GUINNESS

You're going to install a library named guinness. The Guinness library provides the functionality for maintaining a suite of unit tests.

1. From the IDEA project panel, open pubspec.yaml, and add the following line of code in the dependencies:

   ```
   guinness: "0.1.17"
   unittest: "0.11.6+1"
   ```

2. Click Get Dependencies to download guinness to your packages folder.

   ```
   Got dependencies!
   ```

3. From the IDEA project panel, Control-click the tickets folder, select New > Directory, and name the directory test.

4. Control-click the test directory, select New > File, and name the file database_test.dart.

   In the following sections, you'll use the database_test.dart file to execute your test scripts from IDEA.

# COMPOSITION OF A GUINNESS TEST

One of the more helpful aspects of testing frameworks is their ability to facilitate the writing of tests whose output results in concise sentence structures explaining what occurred. This creates a self-documenting trail that enables developers to quickly acquire context as to what the test was originally expecting and why the test failed.

The common nomenclature for test is *spec,* and multiple specs together are referred to as a *suite.*

1. Implement the **Example 13.1** test using the exposed functions from Guinness to help write the test:

   **EXAMPLE 13.1**

   ```
   import 'package:guinness/guinness.dart';


   main() {

     Map student = {'name': null, 'canRead': null};

     describe("8th Grade Student", () {

       beforeEach( () => print('At Start'));
   ```

```
      beforeEach( () {
        student['name'] = "Tommy";
        student['canRead'] = true;
      });

      afterEach( () => print('At Finish'));
      afterEach( () {
        student['name'] = null;
        student['canRead'] = false;
      });

      it("Should Have A Name", (){
        print('--run name test');
        expect(student['name']).toBeNotNull();
      });


      it("Can Read", (){
        print('--run reading test');
        expect(student['canRead']).toBe(true);
        expect(student['canRead']).toBeNotNull();
      });
    });

  }
  //unittest-suite-wait-for-done
  //At Start
  //--run name test
  //At Finish
  //
  //At Start
  //--run reading test
  //At Finish
  //
  //PASS: An 8th Grade Student Should Have A Name
  //PASS: An 8th Grade Student Can Read
  //All 2 tests passed.
  //unittest-suite-success
```

Let's take a look at what you just did:

- You created a variable named `student`. The data assigned to it contains two fields, both with a value of `null`. As is, neither of these values would pass the tests you execute later.

- You invoked the function `describe()`. This function has two parameters: The first is a string value that specifies *the object that is being tested*— in this case, "An 8th Grade Student"; the second parameter is a function argument that executes the tests.

- You invoke two helper functions: `beforeEach()` and `afterEach()`. Neither of these is a test itself. Both functions accept a single function reference that will be invoked either immediately before a test or immediately following each test. These functions give you an opportunity to set up or tear down any dependencies that your test might have. In the example, you are calling each function twice.

  Your first invocation in each pair is a function argument that prints out the execution order. This outputs either "At Start" or "At Finish" in relationship to the execution of the actual test.

  Your second invocation modifies the values of the testable object `student`. The `beforeEach()` instance sets the student to a state that will pass the test, whereas `afterEach()` sets its back to an invalid state. This cycle repeats for each unique test.

- You wrote two tests using the `it()` function. Like its relative `describe()`, this function accepts both a string value and a function. However, the string value here specifies *the results* the expect expression should produce, and the function invokes the logic that produces the results. In this case, you require that the object being tested "Have A Name" and "Can Read."

- Inside the function argument, you invoked the `expect()` function, which accepts a value and returns an `Expect` object. The `Expect` object has numerous variations of the `toBe()` helper function. Most of these functions accept a value, but all the functions test an assumption made upon the value that was first passed into the `expect()` function.

  The `Expect` objects represent the state used to discern the success or failure of a test suite.

  If the results of the expression passed into the `expect()` function match the assumption of the trailing `toBe()` function, the test is considered to have passed. If the assumption is wrong, the test is considered to have failed.

2. Run the code.

   You can see the order of operations clearly in the console output from within `beforeEach()`, `afterEach()`, and `it()`. You'll also notice that the test passes and that the structure of the output sentence is a clear statement describing the object being tested and the assumptions made upon its values.

   Here's an example of the output:

```
//PASS: An 8th Grade Student Should Have A Name
//PASS: An 8th Grade Student Can Read
```

# TESTING MONGO

The goal for the remainder of this chapter is to implement a series of asynchronous tests that validate the expectations you set for the MongoModel class. You'll be instantiating an instance of the MongoModel class that connects to a test database inside MongoDB. It will seed the test database with the initial values, run some tests against the data, and, upon completion, drop the test database.

## SEEDER SPEC

You will now instantiate the dependencies needed to test your MongoModel code.

1. Replace the code in your database_test.dart file with **Example 13.2**:

**EXAMPLE 13.2**

```
import 'package:guinness/guinness.dart'; //test framework
import 'package:tickets/shared/schemas.dart'; //test dtos
import 'package:tickets/db/seeder.dart'; //json file
import 'package:tickets/db/db_config.dart'; //database values
import '../bin/mongo_model.dart';


main() {

  DbConfigValues config = new DbConfigValues();
  MongoModel model = new MongoModel(config.testDbName, config.testDbURI,
  → config.testDbSize);


  //A Test DTO
  RouteDTO routeDTO = new RouteDTO();
  routeDTO.duration = 120;
  routeDTO.price1 = 90.00;
  routeDTO.price2 = 91.00;
  routeDTO.price3 = 95.00;
  routeDTO.seats = 7;
}
```

Let's take a look at what you just did:

- You declared a series of imports. You need access to your DTOs, your JSON file, database configuration values, and, of course, the MongoModel class itself.

- You initialized your database values and your `MongoModel` class. The `config` variable exposes a set of getter properties that modify your previously configured database credentials to point to a new test database named `TicketsTest`.

- You instantiated a new instance of a `RouteDTO`. This is the object that will be used when testing the CRUD actions of your `MongoModel` implementation.

Now that your dependencies are ready for action, you can set up your first spec.

2. Append the code in **Example 13.3** to the end of the `main()` method inside the `database_test.dart` file:

**EXAMPLE 13.3**

```
describe("The Ticket MongoModel", () {
  it('Should populate the Test Database', () async {
    Seeder seeder = new Seeder(config.testDbName,
                              config.testDbURI, config.testDbSeed);
    await seeder.readFile();
    List collection = await model.readCollectionByType( RouteDTO );
    expect(collection.length).toBeGreaterThan(10);
  });
});
```

Let's take a look at what you just did:

- You invoked the method `describe()`. The string value here *describes the object that is being tested.* Any additional expectations that are required to test the described object in this particular context should be included inside the function argument.

- You wrote your first spec using the `it()` method. The string value here specifies *the results* the expect expression should produce. The function then sets up the correct context to evaluate the hypothesis.

  Your expectation is that the route collection will contain more than 10 items. We know that it contains 18 by having looked at the data back in Chapter 7.

  The test function is declared using the keyword `async` because the call itself depends on a Future. The Seeder instance is instantiated, and the `readFile()` method is given time to execute via the `await` keyword. Upon completion, the execution context proceeds.

  You then leveraged the `await` keyword again to assign a value from the asynchronous method `model.readCollectionByType()`.

  You now have your collection to test out your expectation.

- You invoked the `expect()` method, which accepts a value and returns an `Expect` object. In this case, the expectation is that the `collection.length` will be greater than 10. This gives you some flexibility down the road if your seeder data changes.

3. Run `database_test.dart`. You should see the following output:

```
unittest-suite-wait-for-done
PASS: The Ticket MongoModel Should populate the Test Database
All 1 tests passed.
unittest-suite-success
```

In review, you've *described the object that is being tested* and declared *the results the expression should produce*. You'll continue this pattern for the rest of your test suite.

## SPECS AND FUTURES

You are now going to write a test to validate the functionality of the `createByItem()` method on your `MongoModel`. You'll use the instance of `RouteDTO` that you created outside of the describe statement, and you'll ensure it can be persisted inside of MongoDB. Append the code in **Example 13.4** to the bottom of your `describe()` function argument:

**EXAMPLE 13.4**

```
it("should create a route DTO and write to the db", () {
  var originalID = routeDTO.id;
  return  model.createByItem(routeDTO).then(( var dto ) {
    expect(originalID).toBeNull();
    expect(routeDTO.id).toBeNotNull();
    expect(dto.id).toEqual(routeDTO.id);
  });
});
```

Let's take a look at what you just did:

- You constructed your test. You wrote the original id value to a local variable prior to making the create request. You invoked the `then()` method from the futures interface and acquired an instance of the DTO from `MongoModel` after it was written to the database. You then declared your expectations.

- You wrote your second spec using the `it()` method. The string value here specifies the result that the expect expression should produce.

- The `it()` method has built-in support for Dart futures and completers. This allows you to construct asynchronous tests without any additional framework support. In Example 13.4, your result for the `it()` method is a returned `Future` from the model instance.

- Inside your test context, the method `createByItem()` always expects the id value of the DTO to be `null` because it has never been persisted to the database. Upon writing the object to the database, the `MongoModel` returns the same instance to the caller, but with updated values. You wrote some expectations that reflect this scenario, and you checked that the `originalID` is null, that the returned instance's id is not null, and that both active route variables now have matching `id`s.

## SPECS AND ASYNC

You are now going to write a test to validate the functionality of the updateItem() method on your MongoModel. Guinness can also support Dart's built-in support for async because the test function argument is a standard Dart function.

You can use the async keyword to modify the function to behave like an implicit future. First let's take a look at a standard futures-based implementation.

1. Append the **Example 13.5** code to the bottom of your describe() function:

   **EXAMPLE 13.5**

```
var action = "update previous db item, retrieve it to make sure its updated";
it(action, () {
routeDTO.price1=10000.10;
return model.updateItem(routeDTO).then((status) {
    return model.readItemByItem(routeDTO).then((dto){
      expect(status['ok']).toEqual(1.0);
      expect(dto.price1).toEqual(routeDTO.price1);
    });
  });
});
```

Let's take a look at what you just did:

- You wrote your third spec using the it() method.
- You modified the price value on your DTO to 10000.10.
- You immediately returned a future. The future will take the Dart instance of the DTO and update its values in the MongoDB database. The updateItem() method returns only a status object.
- You returned a second future to enable future chaining. This future uses the readItemByItem() that refreshes an object instance from the database.
- You outlined your expectation that the status object has an 'ok' value, and that the returned object has output a price value that matches your local modification.

If you run the code, it will pass, but it's verbose and subjectively difficult to read. Let's use a more idiomatic Dart approach and enable async support.

2. Replace the code from the previous step in your database_test.dart file with the code in **Example 13.6**:

**EXAMPLE 13.6**

```
var action = "update previous db item, retrieve it to make sure its updated";
  it(action, () async {
    routeDTO.price1=10000.10;
    var status = await model.updateItem(routeDTO);
    var dto = await model.readItemByItem(routeDTO);
    expect(status['ok']).toEqual(1.0);
    expect(dto.price1).toEqual(routeDTO.price1);
  });
```

Let's take a look at what you just did:

■ You refactored your third spec by using the async keyword to modify the function argument.

■ You modified the call to model.updateItem() to use the await keyword. This mimics synchronous behavior while allowing asynchronous execution. The response value is assigned to a local variable.

■ You modified the call to model.readItemByItem() to also use the await keyword. The response value is assigned to a local variable.

■ You outlined your expectations to use the local variables as if this were a synchronous call.

The modified code is quite terse and is subjectively easier to read.

3. Run database_test.dart. You should see the following output:

```
unittest-suite-wait-for-done
PASS: The Ticket MongoModel Should populate the Test Database
PASS: The Ticket MongoModel should create a record DTO and write to the db
PASS: The Ticket MongoModel update previous db item, retrieve it to make
→ sure its updated

All 3 tests passed.
unittest-suite-success
```

# READ SPEC

You will now write a test to validate the read functionality of the MongoModel by testing the readItemByItem() and readCollectionByType() methods. One retrieves a specific instance, and the other returns an entire collection.

1. Append the **Example 13.7** code to the bottom of your describe() function argument:

   **EXAMPLE 13.7**

   ```
   it("should retrieve a list of items by the DTO", () {
     return  model.readCollectionByType( RouteDTO ).then(( List<BaseDTO>
       ⇀ aList ) {
       expect(aList.first).toBeAnInstanceOf(RouteDTO);
       expect(aList.length).toBeGreaterThan(10);
     });
   });


   it("will retrieve the item created in the first step", () {
     return  model.readItemByItem(routeDTO).then((BaseDTO dto){
         expect(dto.id).toEqual(routeDTO.id);
       });
    });
   ```

   These tests are actually very similar to some of the tests you've already used. They are broken out into explicit standalone specs. This will ensure that if you start seeing test failures, you have small logical segments tested that allow you to quickly assess where the problem occurs.

2. Run database_test.dart. You should see the following output:

   ```
   unittest-suite-wait-for-done
   PASS: The Ticket MongoModel Should populate the Test Database
   PASS: The Ticket MongoModel should create a record DTO and write to the db
   PASS: The Ticket MongoModel update previous db item, retrieve it to make
     ⇀ sure its updated
   PASS: The Ticket MongoModel will retrieve the item created in the first step
   PASS: The Ticket MongoModel should retrieve a list of items by the DTO

   All 5 tests passed.
   unittest-suite-success
   ```

## DELETE SPEC

You will now write a test to validate the delete functionality of the MongoModel by testing the deleteByItem() method. Append the **Example 13.8** code to the bottom of your describe() function expression:

**EXAMPLE 13.8**

```
it("should delete the route DTO from the DB", () {
  return model.deleteByItem(routeDTO).then( (status) {
    expect(status['ok']).toEqual(1.0);
  });
});
```

Because this is a destructive action, the deleteByItem() method returns a status object. You simply check that status to ensure that the object was deleted.

## DROP DATABASE SPEC

You will now write a test to validate the ability to drop a database using MongoModel by testing the dropDatabase() method. This is important since the first spec you wrote created a new database named TicketsTest. You want to make sure that you clean up after your tests.

1. Append the **Example 13.9** code to the bottom of your describe() function argument:

   **EXAMPLE 13.9**

   ```
   it("should drop the test database", () async {
     Map status = await model.dropDatabase();
     expect(status['ok']).toEqual(1.0);
   });
   ```

   Because this is a destructive action, the dropDatabase() method returns a status object. You simply check that status to ensure that the database was dropped.

2. Run database_test.dart. You should see the following output:

   ```
   unittest-suite-wait-for-done
   PASS: The Ticket MongoModel Should populate the Test Database
   PASS: The Ticket MongoModel should create a record DTO and write to the db
   PASS: The Ticket MongoModel update previous db item, retrieve it to make
   → sure its updated
   PASS: The Ticket MongoModel will retrieve the item created in the first step
   PASS: The Ticket MongoModel should retrieve a list of items by the DTO
   PASS: The Ticket MongoModel should delete the route DTO from the DB
   PASS: The Ticket MongoModel should drop the test database

   All 7 tests passed.
   unittest-suite-success
   ```

## ADDITIONAL TESTS

You just wrote a suite of functional test interacting with your MongoModel. At GitHub, there's an extension of these tests that implements additional test coverage for the TicketingModel class you created. If you're interested in running them, you can take a look at them at:

https://github.com/rightisleft/web_apps_dart/blob/master/test/ticket_model_test.dart.

## SUMMARY

Congratulations, you have taken the first steps to ensure your code continues to function in an explicit, expected manner as you evolve your code base. We've only scratched the surface of unit testing, and I highly suggest taking the time to develop a strong routine around testing your code. Now that you have confidence that your API layer is returning quality results, you're ready to switch gears and dive into front-end development using Dart.

### YOU SHOULD NOW KNOW:

- What a unit test is
- What a spec is
- What a suite is
- What Guinness is, and how it relates to Jasmine
- The relationship between describe() and it()
- The execution order of beforeEach() and afterEach()
- The purpose of the class Expect
- How to write futures-based specs
- How to write specs leveraging async

# CHAPTER 14

# A Web Project
# with Dart

In Chapter 12, you set up the API that will power the Just-In-Time Airlines ticketing application. With that, you will spend the next few chapters familiarizing yourself with Dart as a language for web development. You'll be setting up a landing page using the core `dart:html` library, and then building out the rest of the application using Angular 2 Dart. Let's take a look at getting your landing page up and running.

# PLANNING FOR FRONT-END DEVELOPMENT

When we received the mockups from the client Just-In-Time Airlines back in Chapter 7, you saw that the landing page would be isolated from the rest of the application. The goal is to make a flexible landing page that is isolated from the core ticketing application. This will give the marketing department the flexibility to experiment with different landing pages and offers without affecting the core ticketing platform. It also allows you to take a look at the core dart:html library that is shipped with the Dart SDK.

Over the next few sections, you'll implement a list of discounted flights. Each deal will have the date of travel, a discount price, and deep link into the ticketing application.

## DEVELOPMENT TOOLS

I've talked about a few ways to run Dart in the browser: using Chrome as a browser, using Dartium as a browser, running a server using Pub Serve, running a server using Shelf, and others.

The following list clarifies how you will develop your application from this point through Chapter 16:

- You'll use the Dartium browser to test and debug code using its built-in Dart VM.
- You'll access Dartium's built-in debugger tool.
- You'll serve your content using the IDEA proxy server for Pub.
- You'll run the Shelf router from the previous chapter to expose your data.

**NOTE:** In Chapter 17, you will prepare your app for public consumption by deploying your application to Heroku. At that point, you'll use the task Pub build to compile a JavaScript version of the app and run it locally in a standard browser. Once it's built, you'll be able to serve it using the Shelf static server that was built in Chapter 12.

## DEVELOPMENT LIBRARIES

You'll be starting with a front-end development stack and installing and configuring the support for the following libraries:

- browser will include the client dependencies to execute the dart2js transformer.
- bootjack is a Dart port of the popular Bootstrap UI framework. It adds support for the popular Bootstrap grid system and CSS components. For interactivity it uses Dart instead of JavaScript.
- sass adds a build step for the popular CSS preprocessor. It supports both the sass and scss syntax. The Dart sass library includes a transformer that operates the same way as the dart2js transformer. When a request for a file named main.css is encountered, the Pub server will transform and return the processed output from main.scss. In addition to this server features, all sass/scss files will be transformed and saved during Pub build process. (See the sidebar "Installing and Configuring sass" for more information.)

The following steps acquire and configure the rest of your Dart libraries:

1. From the IDEA project panel, open pubspec.yaml and modify it to match the code in **Example 14.1**:

**EXAMPLE 14.1**

```
name: 'tickets'
version: 0.0.1
description: A ticket commerce application
author: Jack Murphy jack@rightisleft.com
homepage: https://www.rightisleft.com
environment:
  sdk: '>=1.0.0 <2.0.0'
dependencies:
#Server Dependencies
  json_object: "1.0.19"
  mongo_dart: "0.1.46"
  connection_pool: "0.1.0+2"
  dartson: "0.2.4"
  guinness: "0.1.17"
  shelf: '>=0.6.2 <0.7.0'
  shelf_static: "0.2.2"
  shelf_route: 0.13.0
```

```
#Client Dependencies
  bootjack: "0.6.5"
  browser: ">=0.10.0+2 <0.11.0"
  sass: "0.4.2"
transformers:
- dartson
- sass:
  executable: sassc
```

2. Click Get Dependencies to download the libraries to your packages folder.

Got dependencies!

3. Control-click the web folder, select New > File, and name the file `main.dart`.

4. Control-click the web folder, select New > File, and name the file `deals.json`.

5. Control-click the web folder, select New > Directory, and name the directory `styles`.

6. Control-click the styles folder, select New > File, and name the file `main.scss`.

# INTERACTING WITH HTML AND THE DOM

You will build a basic input field to test interactions with the DOM using Dart. To support that, you need an `<input>` field in your HTML. You're going to modify the `index.html` file from Chapter 12.

1. Modify `web/index.html` to match the code in **Example 14.2**:

**EXAMPLE 14.2**

```html
<!DOCTYPE html>
<html>
<head>
  <meta name="viewport" content="width=device-width, initial-scale=1.0">
  <title>JIT Ticket Application</title>
  <link rel="stylesheet" href="packages/bootjack/css/bootstrap.min.css">
  <link rel="stylesheet" href="https://bootswatch.com/flatly/
  → bootstrap.min.css">
  <link rel="stylesheet" href="styles/main.css">
</head>
<body>
<div class="container">
```

```
    <div class="col-xs-12">
      <h1>Ticket Application</h1>
      <a class="btn btn-primary" id="hw">Hello World!</a>
      <hr/>
      <input type="text" class="form-control" placeholder="Blank" />
    </div>
  </div>

  <script type="application/dart" src="main.dart"></script>
  <script src="packages/browser/dart.js"></script>
  </body>
  </html>
```

Each of the HTML elements and scripts in Example 14.2 should look familiar. If you need a refresher on how Dart works in the browser, please refer to Chapter 2. The only variation from any of the previously discussed concepts is the inclusion of CSS files. Here's how you did that:

- `bootstrap.min.css`: You included the CSS required for the Bootjack library.
- `bootstrap.min.css`: This is optional. You extended the default Bootstrap configuration with a custom Bootstrap theme named `flatly`. This file is externally hosted. You have the option to load it off their servers upon page load, or you can download it locally if you want to run it offline. In this example, you will leave it on their servers.
- `main.css`: This is the processed output of the `main.scss` file. This file is generated on the fly by the `sass` transformer library installed earlier in this chapter.

The topic of CSS and SASS will not be covered in this book. Where required, styling code will be included to complete the project.

At a high level, you want an application that is 1170 pixels wide and centered. You'll default to using the bootstrap `col-xs-*` grid prefix. Using the extra small selector will ensure that the page is a consistent width across all browser windows sizes. You can dive into Bootstrap's responsive layout options if you are interested, but this book does not cover them.

You need to add some code to enforce these requirements.

2. Apply the code in **Example 14.3** to your web/styles/main.scss file:

**EXAMPLE 14.3**

```
@import url(https://fonts.googleapis.com/css?family=Roboto);

html, body {
  width: 100%;
  height: 100%;
```

```
      margin: 0;
      padding: 0;
      font-family: 'Roboto', sans-serif;
    }
    .container {
      width: 1170px;
    }
```

Next, you need to construct the base application entry point for your web application.

3. Inside your web/main.dart file, enter the code in **Example 14.4**:

**EXAMPLE 14.4**

```
import 'dart:html';

main() {
  print('This is main.dart from test');
  AnchorElement btn = querySelector('#hw');
  btn.onClick.listen(handleClick);
}


handleClick(Event e) {
  InputElement input = querySelector('input');
  input.value += (e.target as AnchorElement).text;
}
```

Let's take a look at some test output from piecing together the .dart, .scss, and .html files:

4. From the IDEA project panel, open the web folder.

5. Control-click index.html, select Open in Browser, and then select Dartium.

6. Ensure that Dartium opens to the Ticket Application page. Dartium should load an address similar to http://localhost:63342/tickets/web/index.html.

7. Click the Hello World button multiple times to populate the input field with our value.

    Let's do a quick overview of the core concepts by taking a quick look at what you just did. Later in the chapter, you'll do a deep dive into all the components used here.

    ■ querySelector traverses the DOM and uses the DOM string selector syntax to find elements. In this case, you're looking for an element with an ID of value 'hw'.

    ■ AnchorElement is an element exposed by the dart:html library. The dart:html library provides element classes that corresponded to the available tag formats from the HTML specification. In the case of AnchorElement btn, we expect the querySelector() to return an element of type Anchor based off the matching ID.

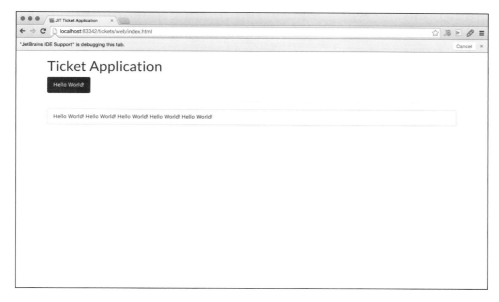

**FIGURE 14.1** An input field populated with event target data

- onClick.listen listens for the click events. The dart:html library works with native Dart streams for event handling. The onClick stream implements the Dart stream interface. This allows you to append event handler functions using the listen method. The handler can then respond to click events.
- handleClick is a function with a method signature parameter named e of type Event. This function executes on each stream event. The event will include a reference to the target element—in this case, an AnchorElement whose text value you append to the end of your InputElement field.

Your screen should now resemble **Figure 14.1**.

# QUERYING THE DOM

Now that you have a basic understanding of how the components work together, let's take a look at some of the core concepts of working with the HTML and the DOM.

## DOM

The Document Object Model (DOM) is the live representation of your page. The DOM exposes the interface that allows you to update the content of your page. At its core, the DOM is a tree structure of objects, with the top-most element being the document object. Each object is a node that can have exactly one or no parent and many children.

## HTML

HTML is a markup language used to define a tree structure that is initially parsed into the DOM. The structure of each tag in the markup language defines the state of the visual representation of the page itself. Each tag pair is considered an element in the structure and derives its functionality from its semantic value.

## TAGS AND ATTRIBUTES

Each element consists of a pair of opening and closings tags represented by a pair of angle brackets that delineate the start and end of an element. Any characters between the angle brackets are considered to be the content of the tag. If the content is in the form of a name–value pair, it is referred to as an attribute.

```
<tag attribute="value"> //opening tag with an attribute
  <child/> //self closing tag named child
</tag> //closing tag
```

The second tag contains a leading forward slash; this slash declares the previous tag pair to be closed. Any tags between the opening tag and the closing tag are considered to be children.

Some elements cannot contain children and are closed using a self-closing tag. Self-closing tags are indicated with a slash prefixing the closing angle bracket.

## SELECTORS

The HTML5 specification has finally provided a standard cross-browser approach for querying elements from the DOM. This query syntax enables us to retrieve elements based on IDs, classes, elements, or custom attribute names. All queries use a string value that queries elements based on the hierarchy in which the selectors are located on the tree.

Because the query syntax is traversing only the DOM, you can use the built-in Chrome tools to test your syntax. You'll use the default selector $() that ships in the Chrome console.

1. From the IDEA project panel, open the web folder.
2. Open index.html.
3. Insert the following code under your <input> element:

```
<!-- Example -->
<span class="economy">
  <span class="economy reclined" id="rowA" ticket="paid">Seat F14</span>
  <span class="economy stable" id="rowB" ticket="unpaid">Seat F15</span>
</span>
```

4. Control-click index.html, select Open in Browser, and then select Dartium.

5. In the Dartium top menu, choose View > Developer > Developer Tools.

6. Select the Console tab.

Let's take a look at how selectors allow you to traverse the DOM and acquire the desired instances of elements.

## ELEMENTS

An *element* is defined by the text immediately following the opening angle bracket, such as <span>. Each tag is required to have at least one attribute. The name attribute is not always a named valued pair.

The query syntax for both elements of a type from the example in step 3 is:

```
$("span") //returns three spans
```

The query syntax for only elements that are children of type span from the above example is:

```
$("span span") //returns only the first nested span
```

## IDS

An *ID* is an attribute designated by a named value pair of id="value" syntax inside an enclosing tag. A tag can have only a single ID at a time. All IDs are intended to be unique instances on the DOM and should not be duplicated.

The query syntax to return the matching ID from the example is:

```
$("#rowA") //returns only the span with Seat F14
```

## CLASSES

A *class* is an attribute designated by named value pair of class="nameA" syntax inside an enclosing tag. A tag can have multiple classes, and a class can exist on multiple elements on the DOM. Its query symbol is the named value prefixed by a dot.

The query syntax for an element of class economy from the example is:

```
$(".economy")   //returns three spans
```

The query syntax for an element of class economy within an element of the class economy is:

```
$(".economy .economy") //returns a nested span with Seat Information
```

The query syntax for any element that is both of class economy and class reclined is:

```
$(".economy.reclined") //returns the span with seat F14
```

### CUSTOM ATTRIBUTES

Custom attributes exist within many front-end frameworks and allow you to apply functionality to a specific element or group of elements by using a unique named attribute.

Where `ticket` is the custom named attribute, the query syntax for an element containing an attribute named `ticket` is:

`$("[ticket]")` *//returns the first match with Seat F14*

The query syntax for an element containing an attribute name of `ticket` with an assigned value of `paid` is:

`$("[ticket='unpaid']")` *//returns the div with Seat F15*

This is only a cursory overview of how selectors work. These selectors are used not only by Dart's querySelector, but also by the DOM, CSS, jQuery, and many other front-end technologies. It's important that you master them, but this starting point should suffice for the remainder of the book.

# BUILDING THE LANDING PAGE

Now that you have a decent understanding of how to work with HTML and the DOM, let's take a look at building the functionality for the landing page.

## CREATE THE BOX TEMPLATE

The landing page will display three boxes advertising discounted travel deals. Each box will contain the following pieces of data:

- Departure city
- Arrival city
- Arrival date
- City description
- Ticket price

You need to update your template to match the specifications to display the three boxes and the fields.

1. Inside the web/index.html file, replace the `<body>` tag with code in **Example 14.5**:

**EXAMPLE 14.5**

```html
<body>
<div class="container">
  <h1>Great Deals</h1>
  <div id="deals" class="row">
    <!-- Target -->
  </div>
</div>

<template>
  <!-- This is a deal box -->
  <div class="col-xs-4">
    <div class="deal-box well clearfix">
      <img/>
      <h3>City</h3>
      <h4>Date</h4>
      <p>Descriptions</p>
      <h5>Price</h5>
    </div>
  </div>
</template>

<script type="application/dart" src="main.dart"></script>
<script src="packages/browser/dart.js"></script>
</body>
```

You now have two key concepts in your index page; let's take a look:

- deals: You created a div with a unique ID. This will be the insertion point at which you'll append all additional element nodes to the tree.

- template: The HTML5 specification introduced a new type of element named *template*. This element is designed for client-side frameworks to clone and re-use. When the browser loads HTML from index.html, the browser won't parse the content inside the template or fetch any of its dependencies.

  The content inside the template is rendered and acted upon only when a client-side script appends the template element to the DOM; at load time, all its internal content is inert.

You'll be grabbing the template element once. For each deal that marketing is running, you'll then create a clone and dynamically populate its properties. Let's go ahead and start coding.

2. Open the web/main.dart file, and modify it to match the code in **Example 14.6**:

**EXAMPLE 14.6**

```dart
import 'dart:html';
import 'dart:async';
import 'package:json_object/json_object.dart';

DocumentFragment _frag;
Element _view;

void main() {
  //Select target where all deals will be added
  _view = querySelector('#deals');

  //Parse Box Template And Store Locally
  _frag = (querySelector('template') as TemplateElement).content;
}
```

Let's take a look at what you just did:

- Element: You created a variable named _view with a class type of Element. You used the querySelector() to assign the result of the response of '#deals'. This is the same deals div mentioned earlier. It will be the container element for all our deal boxes.

- DocumentFragment: You created a variable named _frag of type DocumentFragment. DocumentFragment is a unique kind of element reserved for template elements. These elements have no parent node yet and are not part of the DOM.

Now that you have your template loaded into memory, let's create a class that will handle assigning the elements to typed field names.

3. Add the code from **Example 14.7** to the bottom of the web/main.dart file:

**EXAMPLE 14.7**

```dart
class Deal {
  HeadingElement city;
  ParagraphElement description;
  HeadingElement date;
  HeadingElement price;
  ImageElement image;
```

```
  AnchorElement button;
  DivElement element;

  Deal() {
    element = new Element.div();
    element.nodes.add( _frag.clone(true) );

    city = element.querySelector('h3');
    date = element.querySelector('h4');
    price = element.querySelector('h5');
    image = element.querySelector('img');
    button = element.querySelector('a');
    description = element.querySelector('p');
  }
}
```

Let's take a look at what you just did:

- Deal is a class that has field members mirroring the data structure that was outlined earlier in the chapter. It leverages querySelector() to assign the correct elements to the field members. In this example, the hierarchy is pretty straightforward, but if the template's structure were more complex, it would serve as a great way to encapsulate the view logic.

- element is the actual element that gets added to the DOM. You instantiated a new DivElement, cloned the _frag template from memory, and added the cloned nodes to the element. The element has not been added to the DOM yet because it exists only in memory.

## PROGRAMMATICALLY INSTANTIATE ELEMENTS

You may have noticed that you don't have an anchor element included in the template. Using Dart, you can dynamically create any element and insert it as a child.

Go ahead and append the code from **Example 14.8** to the end of your Deal() constructor method:

**EXAMPLE 14.8**
```
//dynamically add an Anchor Element
button = new Element.a();
button.setAttribute('class', 'btn btn-info');
button.text = "Buy";
element.querySelector('.deal-box').children.add(button);
```

You now have a class that when instantiated will create a new instance that can be appended to the DOM.

## RENDER THE DEALS DATA

You're going to pull your deals data from an external JSON file. Again, the goal of this feature is to allow the marketing content to exist outside the primary application. To support this, you're simply going to use the `HttpRequest` class from the `dart:html` library to load your JSON file.

1. Enter the code from **Example 14.9** into the `web/deals.json` file:

**EXAMPLE 14.9**

```json
{
  "deals": [
    {
      "city_departure" : "SAN",
      "city_arrival" : "SFO",
      "price": "$99.00",
      "description": "King Of Sour Dough!",
      "date": "10/29/2015",
      "image": "http://bit.ly/wiki_sfo",
      "url": "/#/picker/SAN/SFO/2015-10-29/"
    },
    {
      "city_departure" : "SFO",
      "city_arrival" : "LAX",
      "price": "$79.00",
      "description": "Surf & Sand!",
      "date": "10/30/2015",
      "image": "http://bit.ly/wiki_lax",
      "url": "/#/picker/SFO/LAX/2015-10-30/"
    },
    {
      "city_departure" : "SAN",
      "city_arrival" : "SAC",
      "price": "$109.00",
      "description": "Visit The State Capital!",
      "date": "10/31/2015",
      "image": "http://bit.ly/wiki_sac",
      "url": "/#/picker/SAN/SMF/2015-10-31/"
    }
  ]
}
```

Now you need to add the code to parse the JSON data and populate the new elements.

2. Add the code from **Example 14.10** to your web/main.dart file:

**EXAMPLE 14.10**

```
Future render() async {
  String result = await HttpRequest.getString('deals.json');
  JsonObject response = new JsonObject.fromJsonString(result);
  List dealVOs = response.deals;

  dealVOs.forEach((dealVO) {
    Deal aDeal = new Deal();
    aDeal.city.text = '${dealVO.city_departure} to ${dealVO.city_arrival}';
    aDeal.date.text = dealVO.date;
    aDeal.price.text = dealVO.price;
    aDeal.description.text = dealVO.description;
    aDeal.image.src = dealVO.image;
    aDeal.button.href = dealVO.url;
    _view.children.add(aDeal.element);
  });
}
```

Let's take a look at what you just did:

- result: You invoked an asynchronous HttpRequest using the await keyword to mimic synchronous behavior. HttpRequest is part of the dart:html library and allows the client to load external files or data. The get() method makes a call to the local deals.json file to acquire the string result.

- dealVOs: You do not have Dartson in place on the marketing page, so you're using the JsonObject class to expose the json properties using dot syntax. You accessed the array of deals and iterated over them.

> **WARNING:** When working with JsonObject, you don't have strong typing, so a single typo will cause an error on the page.

- aDeal: You instantiated an instance of the Deal class from earlier in the chapter. The Deal class will handle all the cloning and mapping of the template fragment. It will finally expose a new instance on field adeal.element.

- _view: This is the container for all your deals. Once you instantiated a new element and mapped all the properties to the element, you added your new element to its list of existing children.

**FIGURE 14.2** The flight deals page rendered with graphics

## RENDER THE VIEW

So far, you have kept your markup pretty lean and are offloading a lot of the styling to your SCSS file. Let's continue to keep it neat.

1. Append the following to the end of the web/styles/main.scss file:

```
.deal-box {
  h3 { margin-top: 0; }
  img { display: block; width: 100px; height: 66px; float: right; }
  .btn { margin-top: -45px; float: right; }
}
```

2. Append render() to the end of your main() function. If you reload your index page inside Dartium, you should see a page similar to **Figure 14.2** in your browser.

This is the first step in building out your ticketing application. If you click the Buy buttons, you'll notice that they take you to a 404 page. You have yet to build the rest of the application. These should function once the project is complete.

# SUMMARY

Congratulations, you've just finished building your first HTML page in Dart. You should now have a solid understanding of how Dart interacts with the DOM and of how the browser parses HTML to the DOM. The standalone `dart:html` library is extremely powerful and is the foundation for many other high-level client-side frameworks. You'll see many of the concepts used here in the remaining chapters as we review Angular 2 Dart.

## YOU SHOULD NOW KNOW:

- How to listen to stream events from a clicked element
- How to get properties off of a clicked element
- How to apply a Bootstrap theme
- How to configure an SCSS transformer
- How to retrieve an element using `querySelector()`
- How to assign an element to a subclass of its element type
- What the DOM is and how it relates to HTML
- What a tag is
- What an attribute is
- Common selectors for classes, IDs, elements, and attributes
- How to use the `dart:html` version of `HttpRequest`
- Why you should use a template element
- Why a template element doesn't show at first
- How to dynamically create an HTML element

# CHAPTER 15

# Introduction to Angular 2 Dart

Now that you have a good understanding of how Dart, HTML, and the DOM all work together, you can start to dive into Angular 2 and learn about the architecture that will eventually back the client portion of your Just-In-Time Airlines ticketing application.

Angular 2 is the second edition of the popular Angular framework from Google. It was developed to give client developers a consistent approach to building single page applications (SPAs) in the browser. Traditional web applications have centered on the *request* and *response* model to navigate between different pages. Single page applications forgo the full-page reload and instead use JavaScript to make asynchronous requests for data and then modify selected portions of the DOM to reflect the requested change. This allows web application developers to provide an experience on par with that of a desktop or native mobile application.

# THE HISTORY OF ANGULARJS AND ANGULAR DART

The initial goals of the Angular project were focused on the taming of forms and on form validation in the browser. As the project grew, the Angular framework introduced many concepts that web developers found useful for structuring their entire application code. The key features of the Angular framework are its implementation of two-way data binding, dependency injection, module pattern, encapsulation strategies, and directives for DOM modifications. This all-encompassing approach to browser application engineering proved to be popular with programmers accustomed to the fragmented JavaScript landscape with its competing loading patterns, numerous DOM-traversal mechanisms, and overall inconsistency between development approaches.

The Angular 1 project was developed using JavaScript paired with a later introduction of Angular Dart. The Angular Dart project attempted to mirror the core aspects of the JavaScript implementation and did so while also introducing many alternative solutions to the same domain problems.

Right around the time that Angular Dart was hitting version 1.0, the folks inside Google started to look at the long-term roadmap for the Angular project. Although developers had flocked to the V1 Angular projects for both languages, it was becoming apparent that there were core architectural challenges inside the V1 approach of the JavaScript implementation. In comparison, the Angular Dart project had been built with many of the learnings from its JavaScript predecessor. When Google announced its intentions for version 2.0 of its popular framework, it also announced that the migration strategy would be a rewrite of both libraries.

Buried behind the headlines of breaking changes across the JavaScript ecosystem was the subtle realization that many of the approaches in the Angular Dart project were going to be ported to the JavaScript library and formalized in version 2.0 of the Angular framework. Although both projects will see a rewrite, Angular 2 will look very similar to any developer who had the opportunity to work with Angular Dart V1.

# TYPESCRIPT

Due to the size and aspirations of the project, the Angular team wanted to work with an optionally typed language to ensure the best available tooling. To the surprise of many, Google chose to use Microsoft's TypeScript as the core development language. Google announced that TypeScript would allow it to transpile its code out to both JavaScript and Dart. This caught many folks off guard, with some developers concerned that they would be required to work with TypeScript as the base language, and others shocked that Google didn't use Dart.

The reality of the situation is rather nuanced and takes an understanding of the end requirements of the library. Although I'm sure Google would have loved to champion the usage of Dart on such a high-visibility project, the reality is that application development and library development are two very different things.

Dart excels at providing a unified development environment for building complex web applications. A key part of that strategy is the output of tree-shaken optimized JavaScript code. Although that output style is great for building performant web applications, it's horrible for distributing a library that is intended to be used in a different language and, more importantly, that is intended to be read by developers.

TypeScript is an optionally typed superset of JavaScript. It's intended to compile out to human-readable code and is closely tied to the ECMAScript Next roadmap. With TypeScript, Google is able to write the library once. It can then run the code through a TypeScript transpiler that targets Dart and JavaScript with an output of human-readable code. The result of this choice is a V2 strategy for all three languages. Developers can choose what works best for them. We'll be using the Angular2 Dart library in this book.

> **NOTE:** One interesting point of discussion is the active development of the Dart Dev Compiler (DDC) that is slated for release in 2016. I talked about the DDC back in Chapter 1. The DDC will be Dart's attempt at producing human-readable JavaScript. This allows library maintainers to write, test, and debug with all the great tooling for Dart and then deliver readable libraries in JavaScript.

# DEVELOPER PREVIEW WARNING

At the time of this writing, Angular 2 is in what's referred to as a *developer preview* state of development. This means that APIs are in flux, and some concepts might change. After researching the ecosystem, I'm confident that the core theories covered in this book will be useful when Angular 2 enters Beta and finally V2. That being said, the great thing about using Dart and Pub is that you can lock your environment into a point and time using strict library versioning.

I've been working extensively on ensuring that the components featured in the following sections are ready to be introduced and are relatively bug free. I'll be posting updates on Github for future major milestones.

# ANGULAR 2 OVERVIEW

In the following sections, I'll be taking a look at the various concepts that make up the Angular 2 framework. You will set up an *isolated project* to test some of the foundation concepts inside of Angular. You'll build a simple application that tracks the number of mouse clicks on different elements.

Let's start by setting up the temporary project for your new Angular 2 Clicker application.

1. Navigate to the ~/projects/ folder on your operating system.

2. Create a new folder named `clicker`.

3. Open the IDEA Editor.

4. Select Open from either the splash screen or the File menu.

5. In the dialog, navigate to your ~/projects/ folder.

6. Highlight the `clicker` folder, and click Choose to select it.

   This imports your `clicker` project folder into IDEA. Next, you'll create some folders inside your `clicker` project folder.

7. On the left side of the editor in the IDE's Project panel, Control-click the `clicker` folder, and choose New > File. Name the new file `pubspec.yaml`.

8. On the left side of the editor in the IDE's Project panel, Control-click the `clicker` folder, and choose New > Directory. Name the new directory `web`.

9. Control-click the `web` folder, and choose New > File. Name the new file `index.html`.

10. Control-click the `web` folder, and choose New > File. Name the new file `main.dart`.

11. Control-click the `web` folder, and choose New > File. Name the new file `components.dart`.

12. With `pubspec.yaml` still open, enter the following:

```
name: 'clicker'
version: 0.0.1
description: Track all the clickz!
author: Jack Murphy jack@rightisleft.com
homepage: https://www.rightisleft.com
environment:
  sdk: '>=1.0.0 <2.0.0'
dependencies:
#Client Dependencies
  bootjack: "0.6.5"
  browser: ">=0.10.0+2 <0.11.0"
  sass: "0.4.2"
  angular2: "2.0.0-alpha.45"
transformers:
```

```
    - sass
    - angular2:
        entry_points:
            - web/main.dart
    - $dart2js:
        minify: true
        commandLineOptions:
        - --dump-info
        - --show-package-warnings
        - --trust-type-annotations
        - --trust-primitives
```

**13.** From the Pub action bar at the top of the screen, click Get Dependencies:

```
Resolving dependencies...
Got dependencies!
```

## COMPONENTS

An Angular application is made up of a parent component and a tree of its child components. Each component is intended to encapsulate a logical grouping of functionality that
contains a component class, a view decorator, and a component decorator.

Components enable developers to define new HTML elements and their numerous
properties, ranging from DOM structures and events to data assignment, data retrieval, and
business logic. Let's implement two example components and add them to a page. I'll review
what they are made of after they are in place.

**1.** Modify components.dart to match the code in **Example 15.1**:

**EXAMPLE 15.1**

```
import 'package:angular2/angular2.dart';

@Component(
    selector: 'parent'
)
@View(
    directives: const[AChild],
    template:
    '''
    <h2>Parent Count {{ count }}</h2>
    <a-child [name]="'Player A'" (yell)="heard()"></a-child>
```

```
        <a-child [name]="'Player B'" (yell)="heard()"></a-child>
        '''
    )
    class Parent {
      int count = 0;

      void heard() {
        print('--heard--');
        count++;
      }
    }


    @Component(
        selector: 'a-child',
        inputs: const ['name'],
        outputs: const['yell']
    )
    @View(
        directives: const[NgIf],
        template:
        '''
        <div class='row col-xs-6'>
        <h1>Name: {{ name }}</h1>
        <h3>Clicked: {{ count }}</h3>
        <a class='btn btn-info' (click)="talkSelf()">Talk To Self</a>
        <a class='btn btn-info' (click)="talkParent()">Talk To Parent</a>
        <a class='btn btn-info' (click)="talkSelf(); talkParent()">
        → Talk To Self & Parent</a>
        </div>
        '''
    )
    class AChild {
      int count = 0;
```

```
  String name;
  EventEmitter yell = new EventEmitter();

  AChild();

  void talkSelf() {
    print('Self Contained');
    count++;
  }

  void talkParent() {
    print('parent');
    yell.add("MOM!!!!!");
  }
}
```

2. Modify index.html to match the code in **Example 15.2**:

**EXAMPLE 15.2**

```
<!DOCTYPE html>
<html>
<head>
  <meta name="viewport" content="width=device-width, initial-scale=1.0">
  <title>Clicker Application</title>
  <link rel="stylesheet" href="packages/bootjack/css/bootstrap.min.css">
</head>
<body>

<div class="container">
  <parent></parent>
</div>

<script type="application/dart" src="main.dart"></script>
<script src="packages/browser/dart.js"></script>
</body>
</html>
```

**FIGURE 15.1**
The default browser
state for the Clicker
application

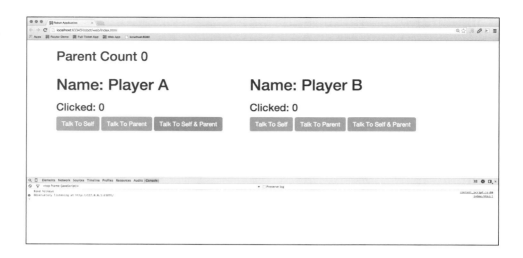

3. Modify main.dart to match the code in **Example 15.3**:

**EXAMPLE 15.3**

```dart
import 'package:angular2/angular2.dart';
import 'package:angular2/bootstrap.dart';
import 'package:angular2/router.dart';
import 'components.dart';

void main() {
  var appComponent = Parent;
  var inejectableBindings = [ ROUTER_BINDINGS, bind(APP_BASE_HREF).
toValue('/'),
    bind(LocationStrategy).toClass(HashLocationStrategy)];

  bootstrap(appComponent, inejectableBindings);
}
```

4. Run your application by right-clicking index.html and selecting Open In Browser > Dartium.
Upon launch, you should see a screen similar to **Figure 15.1** in your browser:

   ■ If you click the Talk To Self button for Player A or Player B, you'll see the child's clicked count increase.

   ■ If you click the Talk To Parent button for Player A or Player B, you'll see the parent count increase.

   ■ If you click the Talk To Self & Parent button for Player A or Player B, you'll see the corresponding child's clicked count and the parent count increase.

You've instantiated three components: one `Parent` component and two instances of the `AChild` component. I'll break down the parts of this very basic Angular application over the next few sections. Afterwards, you'll get back to building your Just-In-Time Airlines ticketing application.

### COMPONENT DECORATORS

Components are structures that enable developers to create custom HTML elements and to instantiate an extendable class instance that controls the element's business logic.

A *component decorator* is where you define the new tag, declare the required interface for the tag, and bind attributes on the tag to component classes' instance variables.

---

**METADATA ANNOTATIONS**

The Dart language has built-in support for metadata annotations. Metadata annotations allow a user to assign values to the compile-time constants of a program's structure (library fields, class fields, and so on). Angular makes heavy use of these to ensure that corresponding application configuration code is available immediately at run time. This helps the framework avoid race conditions between when a user provides the configuration information and when Angular tries to modify the asset. Metadata annotations must point to compile-time constants variables or compile-time constants constructors.

https://www.dartlang.org/docs/dart-up-and-running/ch02.html#metadata

---

Component decorators use Dart's annotation syntax to allow you to declare the fields on a `ComponentMetadata` class. Let's take a look at some of those fields:

- **Selector:** Declares the named string value of the new tag. When an element with the assigned name is found on the DOM, Angular will instantiate the component.

```
@Component(
  selector: 'a-child',
  ...
)
```

- **Inputs:** A list of field names that are expected as both an attribute on a tag and a field on the component object.

```
@Component(
  ...
  inputs: const ['name'],
  ...
)
```

We'll look at these in depth in the section "Data Binding." For now, let's take a look at how an input value is implemented across the various consumers:

- **Field Instance:** When a value is included in the inputs list, a variable of the same name *must* also be declared on the component class. The following is an example from the AChild class:

```
//input value 'name;'
//is also field instance on class AChild
class AChild {
    String name;

    ...
}
```

- **Getter:** Fields will be retrieved inside the template using the double curly brace notation. The template will reflect the value of the field instance from the component class. The following is an example from the AChild view template:

```
//will show value from corresponding Field Instance of 'name'
<h1>Name: {{ name }}</h1>
```

- **Setters:** Properties bind the *named attribute* assignment on the *component selector tag* to the *field instance* using square bracket notation. The following is an example of setting a value on the AChild tag from the view template on the component Parent:

```
//will assign an expression value to a field declared as 'name'
//'Player B' value is assigned to the component class instance 'name'
    <a-child [name]="'Player B'" ... "></a-child>
```

- **Outputs:** A list of field name values that expose an available event name on the element and associate the name with a matching EventEmitter field instance on the component class object.

```
@Component(
    ...
    outputs: const['yell']
)
```

Let's take a look at how an output value is then implemented across various consumers:

- **Field Instance:** A value that's included in the outputs list must also be declared on the component class using standard Dart variable declaration and instantiation syntax. The field instance will be an instance of EventEmitter. The EventEmitter is a wrapper for the Dart Stream class and behaves similarly. The following is an example from the AChild component:

```
// variable name matches the List value
class AChild {
    ...
    EventEmitter yell = new EventEmitter();
    ...
}
```

- **Event Trigger:** When you want to trigger an output event to be heard by a parent component, you call the add() method on the EventEmitter instance. The following is an example from the AChild component where you explicitly trigger a custom event from within the component:

```
void talkParent() {

  ..

  yell.add('MOM!!!!!');

}
```

- **Event Listener:** When you want to listen to a custom output event from a child component, you use parentheses around the output field name and provide an expression to be evaluated on any occurrence. The following is an example of listening for a yell output event from the AChild component inside the Parent template.

```
// yell is a named variable instance on the Component class

// heard() exists in the parent component scope

// heard() will be invoked on any event from yell

<a-child ... (yell)="heard()"></a-child>
```

## VIEW DECORATORS

In a second usage of annotations, Angular expects a view annotation to help decorate the view aspects of the component. The View decorator is responsible for defining aspects of the component that include the HTML, CSS, and DOM traversal and modifications.

- template **and** templateUrl: The ViewMetadata class accepts either a string containing raw HTML or a string containing a URL pointing to an HTML template. The following is an example of an inline string template using Dart's multiline string syntax:

```
@View(

  ...

  template:
    '''

    <div class='row col-xs-6'>
    <h1>Name: {{ name }}</h1>
    <h3>Clicked: {{ count }}</h3>
    <a class='btn btn-info' (click)="talkSelf()">Talk To Self</a>
    <a class='btn btn-info' (click)="talkParent()">Talk To Parent</a>
    <a class='btn btn-info' (click)="talkSelf(); talkParent()">
      Talk To Self & Parent
    </a>
    </div>
    '''

  ...

)
```

- styles and styleUrl: The ViewMetadata class accepts either a string containing raw CSS or a string containing a URL pointing to a CSS file.

  ```
  @View(
    ...
    styleUrl: "package:clicker/path/to/style/file.css"
    ...
  )
  ```

- encapsulation: This is an object that accepts the assignment of an enum of the same name. The available options trigger either the enabling or the disabling of the Shadow DOM. If enabled, the component will be rendered in its own encapsulated Shadow DOM element, with its own scoped CSS and element tree. The following example tells Angular *not* to use the Shadow DOM for a View template:

  ```
  @View(
    ...
    encapsulation: ViewEncapsulation.None,
    ...
  )
  ```

- directives: The ViewMetadata class accepts a list of directive names that get exposed to the template's scope. A directive is a class that exposes logic that modifies the DOM and modifies the variable scope within the selected element tree. To enable a directive to be used in a specific view, the directive itself must be injected in the view. The following code exposes the directives NgIf and NgSwitch to the template defined within the same view:

  ```
  @View(
    //exposes 2 directives to the template
    directives: const [NgIf, NgSwitch],
    ...
  )
  ```

**NOTE:** NgIf and NgSwitch are covered later in the chapter.

## COMPONENT CLASS

The Component class is where you implement the business logic for the component. If both the view decorator and the component decorator are in place, the component will be a Dart class of the naming of your choice. Once declared, it must fulfill the contract requirements from its decorators.

*Templates* from the view decorator will operate in the same scope as your Component class instance, exposing both its variables and its methods from the instance.

*Inputs* defined on the component decorator are required *fields* on the component class. The following is a Component class example from the AChild component:

```
...
class AChild {
  int count = 0;
  String name;
  EventEmitter yell = new EventEmitter();

  Achild();

  void talkSelf() {
    print('Self Contained');
    count++;
  }

  void talkParent() {
    print('parent');
    yell.add('Bubble Up!');
  }
}
```

## DATA BINDING

Data binding is the mechanism in which we keep data in sync amongst various components. Historically, binding data in the DOM has required developers to set up programmatic listeners to handle change events.

Input and output bindings expose a format allowing to you explicitly control the relationship between three structures:

- A tag's element attributes
- A component decorator's list of inputs and outputs
- A component class's field instances

### INPUT BINDING AND FIELDS

When you see the *square bracket syntax* on an element in Angular 2, it should inform you that you are *assigning a value*. This syntax enables a one-way flow of data from the parent to the child.

- The component class's field instances are always exposed to the associated template.

```
class Example {
    String time;
}
```

- The Component inputs value binds a tag's matching attribute to a component class's field instance.

```
@Component(
  inputs: const['time']
)
```

- An element attribute allows a template to set the value of a field via an input binding using square bracket syntax.

```
<example [time]='240'></example>
```

### OUTPUT BINDING AND EVENT EMITTERS

When you see the *round bracket syntax* on an element in Angular 2, it should inform you that you are *listening for an output event*.

When you want data to come out of a component, you will use output events:

- The Component outputs value binds a tag's matching attribute to a component class's field instances.

```
@Component(
  outputs: const['sound']
)
```

- The component class's field instances are now exposed on the element.

```
class Example {
    EventEmitter sound = new EventEmitter();
}
```

- The element attribute allows a template to *listen* for an event to be emitted via output event binding using round bracket syntax. It accepts an expression that is executed on each event occurrence.

```
<example (sound)='handleSound()'></example>
```

### TWO-WAY DATA BINDING

When you see both *square* and *round bracket syntax* on an element in Angular 2, it should inform you that you are implementing two-way data binding. For the most part, this is frowned upon in Angular 2, but it is exposed in a few cases, such as form inputs with NgModel. NgModel is primarily used to bind forms to model data.

```
//where item is a Dart class with a field of String name
<input [(ng-model)]="item.name"></input>
```

## DEPENDENCY INJECTION

Within an application, it's sometimes useful to share a single instance of a class across multiple consumers. Dependency injection (DI) is a design pattern that helps alleviate the need to instantiate the same object across multiple classes. DI offloads the object creation and then makes the instance available through various service location implementations.

Angular exposes the service locator functionality in two primary locations, through an actual injector instance or through the Component class's constructor method signature.

The `Injector` class instance is instantiated and bound by default at application startup.

Let's use the method signature approach to acquire the actual instance of the injector and then retrieve another default service, named `Router`.

```
class ExampleComponent {

  Router router;
  Injector injector;
  ...

  ExampleComponent(Injector this.injector) {
    router = injector.get(Router);
  }
  ...
}
```

As you can see in the example, you never need to pass an argument to the `ExampleComponent` constructor in order to acquire the injector instance. The DI system goes out and locates the instance based off the `Type` and then provides it for you. Once you have an instance of the actual `Injector`, you use the same `Injector` service that is abstracted to acquire the singleton instance of `Router`.

You can make your own classes available for DI by leveraging the `bind(T).toClass(Class)` function to acquire a `BindingBuilder` instance method as an argument for `bootstrap()` on application start.

> **NOTE:** All classes that are available for DI should be annotated with `@Injectable()` to enable the Dart transformer to preprocess the code to ensure proper size and performance.

## DIRECTIVES

A directive is a component with no programmatically defined view. Instead, their view is defined by the element onto which the directive is applied. The applied element and its corresponding sub-tree become the template instance. This makes directives ideal for declaring reusable chunks of DOM logic. Angular 2 ships with multiple directives that are used to conditionally modify the DOM from within other views.

To declare a directive, you use Dart's annotation syntax to annotate the `DirectiveMetadata` class. Let's take a look at an included directive to see how the Angular team writes a directive:

```
@Directive(
  selector: "[ng-if]",
  inputs: const ["ngIf"]
)
class NgIf {
  ViewContainerRef _viewContainer;
  TemplateRef _templateRef;
  bool _prevCondition = null;
  NgIf(this._viewContainer, this._templateRef);

  set ngIf(newCondition) {
    if (newCondition &&
      (isBlank(this._prevCondition) || !this._prevCondition)) {
        this._prevCondition = true;
        this._viewContainer.createEmbeddedView(this._templateRef);
    } else if (!newCondition &&
      (isBlank(this._prevCondition) || this._prevCondition)) {
        this._prevCondition = false;
        this._viewContainer.clear();
    }
  }
}
```

The structure of an `@Directive` annotation should look very familiar to you. It shares the same properties as an `@Component` annotation but without an `@View`.

In the previous example, the `properties` `ngIf` value is bound to a corresponding setter that is implemented using Dart's setter syntax on the component class. This allows the selector to be both a `selector` and a `property` that can accept an expression as an argument.

## NGIF

The `NgIf` directive allows you to apply conditional logic and remove elements from the DOM. If the expression that is passed in evaluates to `true`, a clone of the element will be inserted into the previous location.

```
<!--This will not show -->
<div *ng-if="1 + 1 == 2">Your math is good!</div>
<!--This will not show -->
<div *ng-if="1 + 1 == 5">Your math is bad...</div>
```

Directives prefixed with a *, such as `*ng-if` and `*ng-for`, are template directives that modify the DOM and expose scope to the sub-tree. The * symbol is an abstraction of the template syntax. The * prefix allows IDEs and analyzers to easily identify Angular components but also maintains the terse syntax for writing directives.

As you remember from Chapter 14, template elements must be added programmatically to the DOM. The following three examples are exactly the same:

```
<div *ng-if="1 + 1 == 2">Your math is good!</div>
<div template="ng-if 1 + 1 == 2">Your math is good!</div>
<template [ng-if]="1 + 1 == 2"><div>Your math is good!</</div></template>
```

## NGFOR

The `NgFor` directive allows you to instantiate a clone of the associated element for each item in a collection of data. The current item from the collection is assigned to a scope variable with a prefixed hash symbol. This will expose the variable with the scope of the instantiated element's sub-tree.

```
<!-- items = ['alpha', 'beta', 'charlie', 'delta', 'foxtrot'] -->
<li *ng-for="#item of items; #i = index">{{ item + " " + index.toString() }}</li>

<!- results in -->
<li>alpha 1<li>
<li>beta 2<li>
<li>charlie 3<li>
<li>delta 4<li>
<li>foxtrot 5<li>
```

## NGCLASS

The `NgClass` directive allows you to apply classes to a selected element. The behavior changes depending on which type of value the expression evaluates to:

- String instances will result in a traditional CSS selector being applied to the element.
  ```
  <div class="robot" [ng-class]="flying">
      Beep Beep Boop
  </div>
  ```

- List instances will result in each string value in the list being applied as a traditional CSS selector using a FIFO hierarchy.

```
<!-- List states = ["hovering", "flying", "warping"] -->
<div class="robot" [ng-class]="states">
    Beep Beep Boop
</div>
```

- Map instances will be interpreted as a key–value pair where the key is applied if the value expression result is a Boolean of true.

```
<!-- Boolean hasFuel = true -->
<!-- You would only want the falling class applied if the robot had no fuel
-->
<div class="robot" [ng-class]="{falling: hasFuel == false}">
    Beep Beep Boop
</div>
```

### NGSWITCH

The NgClass directive allows you to implement multiple templates and swap between them when a specified value is matched. The NgSwitch directive is actually a combination of three separate directives:

- ng-switch: This directive is applied to the outermost element. Its sole purpose is to evaluate the expression that provides the value informing the selected state.

```
<!-- List states = ["hovering", "flying", "warping"] -->
<div class="robot" [ng-switch]="states.first">
    <!-- -->
</div>
```

- ng-switch-when: This directive can be used only when applied to a child element of ng-switch. The ng-switch-when directive accepts a single value. When the supplied value matches that argument supplied to the parent ng-switch directive, the element becomes visible. If it does not match, the element remains hidden.

```
<!-- List states = ["hovering", "flying", "warping"] -->
<div class="robot" [ng-switch]="states[1]">
    <hover-suite [ng-switch-when]="hovering"></hover-suite >
    <flying-suite [ng-switch-when]="flying"></flying-suite >
    <warping-suite [ng-switch-when]="warping"></warping-suite >
</div>
```

- ng-switch-default: This directive can be used only when applied to a child element of ng-switch. The ng-switch-default directive accepts no arguments. An element with this directive is displayed only if none of the ng-switch-when directives provide a matching value to the parent expression.

```
<!-- List states = ["flying", "warping"] -->
<div class="robot" [ng-switch]="states.first">
    <hover-suite ng-switch-default></hover-suite >
    <flying-suite [ng-switch-when]="flying"></flying-suite >
    <warping-suite [ng-switch-when]="warping"></warping-suite >
 </div>
```

### NGSTYLE

The NgStyle directive allows you to set an element's style programmatically. NgStyle uses a map that is interpreted as a key–value pair where the key is a style selector string and the value is an expression that provides the corresponding styling.

```
<!-- String locations = ["left", "center", "right"] -->
<div class="robot" [ng-style]="{ "text-align": direction[2] }">
    <!-- I will render to the right -->
    Beep Beep Boop
 </div>
```

## SUMMARY

Congratulations, you have taken the first steps to mastering Angular 2 Dart. You've successfully built a simple application with multiple components, passed data in and out of components, and looked at a number of the subsystems that power the Angular framework. In the next chapter, you'll use Angular 2 to finish the client portion of the Just-In-Time Airlines ticketing application.

### YOU SHOULD NOW KNOW:

- Why Angular Dart is used
- Where Angular Dart is in its development cycle
- The relationship between Angular Dart, Angular JS, and TypeScript
- The structure of an Angular application
- What a component decorator is
- What a view decorator is
- How a component class is used
- The difference between a component and directive
- How directives use the HTML template element
- How to use Angular Dart's built-in directives

# CONGRATULATIONS!

You've successfully worked through the printed material of this book, but that doesn't mean you're finished. As you saw in Chapter 15, you've just begun to scratch the surface of working with Angular 2. You still need to build out the client for your Just-In-Time Ticketing application, and then integrate it with the back end. In order to provide the most up-to-date material, I've posted Chapters 16 and 17 online. Refer to the "Online Content" section in the "Introduction" for more information on accessing these online chapters.

Good luck on the rest of your journey with Dart and Angular 2.

# INDEX